TABLE OF CONTEN

NOTES FOR A MAGAZINE

I am thrilled to present you with this second installment of work from the Southern Lesbian Feminist Activist Herstory Project. In *Sinister Wisdom 98: Landykes of the South*, the Southern Lesbian Feminist Activist Herstory Project presents interviews, stories, memories, poems, and reports about lesbian land communities in the South from 1969 until the present.

In the pages of *Sinister Wisdom 98: Landykes of the South*, some of my favorite lesbian feminists make marquee appearances: Barbara Deming, Andrea Dworkin, Merril Mushroom, Amoja Three Rivers, and others. The stories of *Landykes of the South* ultimately are not about outsized, charismatic individuals. They are stories about communities where individuals gather to create something greater and more meaningful than any one person.

Sinister Wisdom 98: Landykes of the South is narrated skillfully and organized to evoke Southern lesbian land communities. This is an issue that simultaneously educates and delights. If you are like me, you will be riveted reading these stories about lesbian landykes and learn an extraordinary amount of new information about lesbian-feminism, land communities, and the visions that womyn brought to community building. Perhaps equally important to the inspiration that these stories offer are the clear-eyed assessments of challenges and frustrations in building land communities. These are powerfully human stories that help us all understand more about lesbian-feminism and where—and how—we live our lives.

From this issue of *Sinister Wisdom*, the complexities of lesbian identities and lesbian-feminist political actions emerqe. The stories in these pages capture many people's lives and modes of finding ways to live in the world with integrity, conviction, passion, and pleasure. *Sinister Wisdom 98: Landykes of the South* also contributes to the important work of documenting the history of lesbian-feminism—and lesbian separatism. Discussing, debating, analyzing, and arguing about lesbian separatism has been an important topic for *Sinister Wisdom* since the journal began. I am pleased to see the conversation continuing with this issue.

I want to praise all of the women working on the Southern Lesbian Feminist Activist Herstory Project and Womonwrites, the Southern gathering of women writers that nurtures and supports this project. These great writers, activists, and *bon vivants* preserve lesbian lives through storytelling, oral herstory interviews, and archival preservation. I salute them for their work.

I also want to thank Rose Norman who has been my primary contact and liaison through the process of these two special issues. Rose is an extraordinarily smart, funny, hard-working, compassionate, thoughtful, and committed lesbian; it is a pleasure to work with her. Thank you, Rose, for the work you are doing on *Sinister Wisdom*—and a myriad of other projects that benefit lesbians.

If you love this issue of *Sinister Wisdom* (and I hope you will!) please consider making a generous gift to *Sinister Wisdom*. I have four fabulous issues of *Sinister Wisdom* planned for 2016, but we can only publish and distribute these issues with your support. *Sinister Wisdom* will have a special fall fundraising campaign in October and November with an ambitious fundraising goal, but you can give to support *Sinister Wisdom* at any time online at www. SinisterWisdom.org/donate or by mailing a check payable to *Sinister Wisdom* to *Sinister Wisdom*, PO Box 3252, Berkeley, CA 94703.

Please note the subscription rates for *Sinister Wisdom* increase slightly in January of 2016. You can lock in a two-year subscription for only $50 (in the United States) or a one-year subscription for only $34 (in the United States) before the end of December. Take action now and save money in the future! You'll be glad you did.

In sisterhood,

Julie R. Enszer, PhD
Fall 2015

NOTES FOR A SPECIAL ISSUE
LANDYKES OF THE SOUTH:
WOMEN'S LAND GROUPS AND LESBIAN
COMMUNITIES IN THE SOUTH

"Lesbiana
It became my country,
a space where I belonged,
a territory beyond borders
made up of islands
linked to each other
by love, ideas and political affinities."

Myriam Fougère, *Lesbiana: A Parallel Revolution* (2012)

It was the 1970s. Lesbians owning land together was a new concept. Second-wave feminism was new. National feminist organizations were new, and were not welcoming out Lesbians. It was only a few years after Stonewall. Every woman was finding her own path.

Some of us stepped onto the utopian, arduous, and, in some ways, ethereal path of the women's (womyn's, wimmin's) land movement, a world evoked in the lines quoted above from Myriam Fougère's documentary about that time, a time when *Lesbian* was spelled with a capital "L" because it meant a member of a nation, a tribe. Small groups of Lesbians began to find ways of acquiring land where they could live the ideals of the movement. How they achieved this vision has varied as much as the women themselves varied. Some had inherited lands or had the resources to simply buy land, while others worked collectively to borrow money or raise funds through a charitable group. In 1994, when Shewolf published her first *Shewolf's Directory of Wimmin's Lands and Lesbian Communities,* now in its sixth edition (2013–2016, see story, p. 113), fifty land groups were included. Eighteen of these were in the South. By 1996, Landyke Gatherings (*Landyke* capitalized for the same reason as *Lesbian*) started at In Touch in Virginia and have continued to meet every two or three years.[1] The first seven gatherings were in Southern states.[2]

Sinister Wisdom 98: Landykes of the South is the second special issue of *Sinister Wisdom* featuring memoirs, interviews, essays, and artifacts from the Southern Lesbian Feminist Activist Herstory Project, a project of Womonwrites, the Southeast Lesbian Writers' Conference (womonwrites.wordpress.com). While our focus here is on land groups in Southern states (Alabama, Arkansas, Florida, Georgia, Kentucky, Louisiana, Mississippi, Missouri, North Carolina, Tennessee, Virginia, and West Virginia), we have also attempted to provide broader context for this nationwide movement. The main goal of our Herstory Project is to fill a gap left in the history of the second-wave women's movement by collecting the stories of the many Lesbian-feminist activists living in Southern states. Stories and histories of many Southern Lesbians-feminists are missing from the burgeoning oral history projects documenting histories of feminism in the 1970s and the 1980s or in LGBT oral history projects.[3] While excellent scholarly

---

1 Landyke Gatherings are just what they sound like, gatherings of Lesbians who live on womyn's lands all over the United States, including people who don't live in a Lesbian land community but identify as Landykes. That term may have first appeared in print when Jae Haggard, now editor of *Maize*, used it in 1995. Sociologist Landyke Sine Anahita (formerly of Bold Moon womyn's land in North Carolina) used the term in a 2004 scholarly article, "Rivers of Ideas, Participants, and Praxis: The Benefits and Challenges of Confluence in the Landdyke Movement," *Research in Political Sociology* 13 (2004): 13–46; and again in 2009, "Nestled into Niches: Prefigurative Communities on Lesbian Land," *Journal of Homosexuality* 56.6 (2009): 719–737. Dr. Anahita spells it with two d's, as does the Landdykes online discussion group. After a discussion on the Landdykes e-list, we have used Jae Haggard's spelling, with one d, on the grounds that, as Shewolf wrote, "it makes it hard to separate the land from the dykes."

2 In 1996 and 1997 at In Touch (now called CampOut), 1998 at Sugarloaf, 1999 and 2000 at SPIRAL, 2001 at Camp Sister Spirit, and 2002 again at SPIRAL.

3 Rachel Blau DuPlessis and Ann Snitow, *The Feminist Memoir Project: Voices from Women's Liberation* (New York: Three Rivers Press, 1998), Rosalyn Baxandall and Linda Gordon, *Dear Sisters: Dispatches from the Women's Liberation Movement* (New York: Basic Books, 2001), Twin Cities GLBT Oral History Project, *Queer Twin Cities* (Minneapolis: University of Minnesota Press, 2010).

work has been done on the South as an important site of activism,[4] many stories of Lesbian-feminist activism remain to be told.

For some early women's liberationists in the first consciousness-raising groups, forming a women's land group was an outcome of the process, putting theory into action (see p. 19 for Corky Culver's story). Some Lesbians came out in the counterculture's back-to-the-land movement, some waking up to feminism after moving to the country with a mixed group or male partner (see "Arkansas Land," p. 36). Our collection of Landyke stories begins in 1969 when Corky Culver's consciousness-raising group in Florida, possibly the first Lesbian land group in the country, began to look for land. We chose to end the storytelling at the end of the twentieth century in 1998 with Maat Dompim (see "A Great Big Women of Color Tent," p. 150), but the Landyke movement continues in some form to this day. Reflecting this, our timeline includes communities started up to 2012 (see "Women's Land in Southern States," p. 177).

At heart, Lesbian-feminism is part of every woman's land story in this issue, and for some, Lesbian separatism was a theme, if not a bone of contention. The topic of Lesbian separatism could be an entire chapter in and of itself. In brief, some land groups professed to be separatist from inception, while others became separatist to varying degrees over time. Some groups mandated no men on the land at all, which could be difficult when it came to certain jobs or equipment. They believed they could figure it out, and do it better, safer, or more respectfully than men. Some allowed limited male presence; some allowed men only at specific times and in specific places, to stay connected with sons, brothers, or fathers. Others

4 See, for example, *Rebels, Rubyfruits, and Rhinestones: Queering Space in the Stonewall South*, edited by James T. Sears (New Brunswick, NJ: Rutgers University Press, 2001) and Carol Giardina's *Freedom for Women: Forging the Women's Liberation Movement: 1953-1970*, which gives more attention to Southern activism than do most histories of the movement (Gainesville, FL: University Press of Gainesville, 2010).

tried to have as little contact as possible with the heteropatriarchy, even while off the land. Often the issue of separation and degrees of such was a matter for endless processing. Landykes were creating something larger, beyond a couple or a family. They attempted to live out egalitarian and ecological principles, which they saw as the core of female culture. They attempted this within sometimes stark financial, cultural, and psychological limitations.

Along with new political awareness, new lifestyles, new environments, new families of choice, etc., many Lesbian-feminists took new names. Often these names were associated with nature or spirituality, and usually they were very meaningful. Some women took new names, some were given new names, and some had a vision or highly significant experience. Sometimes a new name was taken in fun or just grabbed out of thin air. Some were bestowed with ritual and ceremony, and some were transitory. Some women from those early days retain their chosen names to this day, and some even have legally changed their names.

This era, the latter third of the twentieth century, predated the internet. It cannot be overstated how hard it was for Lesbians to find each other before the networking and consciousness raising that came with the women's movement, and it cannot be overstated how hard it was for Landykes to connect when we were scattered across distances with no email, no internet, and sometimes no electricity or phone. When the internet came to rural America, it was strictly dial-up. These wimmin were stitched together by methods and institutions of their own making.

Traveling dykes, idealistic nomads for a time, were an important link between Landykes, bringing news and controversies to the lands they visited. Often, they were looking for a place to settle, and contributed skills and labor to the lands they visited. They shared what life was like where they had been visiting, as well as their own strong feminist opinions of how each land group should be living. These travelers often challenged communities to change, or pushed them to greater clarity of vision and methods. More of their personal stories need to be told as well (see Naj McFadden's story, p. 121).

In putting together this special issue, we were struck once again by the overwhelming whiteness of our participants. Arco Iris and Maat Dompim (see articles pp. 43 and 150) were the only women of color land groups we could find in the South, and we found few individuals of color participating in white land groups. Although our focus is on the South, we reached out nationwide to individuals, groups, organizations, and publications that we hoped might be helpful, asking for assistance in reaching possible ethnically diverse participants. Those few who responded put out our call in their publications, networks, lists, websites, and other means of communication. We followed up on every lead. The consensus of the responses was that Landykes of color were few, and women of color land groups in the South almost nonexistent.

This should not have been surprising, especially given the time period covered. Women of color still struggled to secure equal rights as citizens. Black women worked together with Black men to end racism, and Lesbians of color faced the additional challenges of misogyny and homophobia. White women were learning to recognize their own internalized racism, but often women of color doubted white women's commitment to ending it. While many white Southern Lesbian-feminists had a growing consciousness around issues of racism—some of us were very active in antiracism politics and actions—this was not always the primary focus for others. They may have wanted, even craved, more ethnic diversity, but creating the circumstances for this to happen was not something they were skilled at doing, and often they unintentionally perpetuated barriers to Black women and women of color. In addition to getting along with each other, Lesbians were surrounded by and contending with the all-pervasive lesbophobic and racist patriarchy.

Many economic and cultural issues also come into play. Southern Lesbians of African descent often came from families who had been poor and oppressed in the rural South, and they were seeking opportunities for upward mobility through more education and better jobs in the cities. Economically and culturally, their movement was toward the city, not living isolated or under "rustic" conditions. For some, living in the country in relative isolation did not seem safe or desirable. The commonality of lesbianism was simply not enough.

Joyce Cheney started traveling to women's land groups and collecting their stories in 1981, eventually publishing *Lesbian Land,* essays about twenty-six different sites (including one in Denmark), as well as interviews with and essays by Lesbians interested in women's land (1985). Before the publication of this invaluable book, Lesbians looking for land communities looked where many searched for all things Lesbian—in *Lesbian Connection.*[5] *LC* occasionally published a national listing of lands, based on what communities sent them, starting in the late 1970s. *Woman Spirit Magazine* (1975-1985) and *Country Women* (1972-1980) were also important sources of information for Landykes.

Lee Lanning, Nett Hart, and later Jae Haggard, although not Southern dykes, provided a great deal of financial and other support for Lesbians living on land through Lesbian Natural Resources (LNR). LNR funded many projects, purchased equipment, and referred garden and building interns who came to work and live on Southern Lesbian land (see LNR, p. 173). They also published *Maize Magazine*, which continues to enrich the lives of country dykes as a forum for information resources and myriad connections. Currently edited by Jae Haggard at Outland near Serafina, New Mexico, and supported by a working cohort of

---

5 For more information about *LC*, see www.LConline.org or www.facebook.com/LConline.

amazing country dykes from around the United States, *Maize* has published over a hundred issues.[6]

In the 1990s in Louisiana, Shewolf (Dr. Jean Boudreaux) began compiling *Shewolf's Directory of Wimmin's Lands and Lesbian Communities*. Of the twenty-six sites described in *Lesbian Land*, only five remain in the current edition of *Shewolf's Directory* (sixth edition), three of them in the South: the North Forty, also known as Long Leaf, in Florida; The Pagoda in Florida; and Silver Circle in Mississippi. In that latest *Directory*, more land groups and Lesbian communities are located in Southern states than anywhere else in the country: one each in Alabama, Arkansas, and Mississippi; two each in Kentucky, North Carolina, Virginia, and West Virginia; three in Missouri; four in Tennessee; and a dozen in Florida. With months of effort to create an inclusive timeline, we found about fifty named lands or communities created in the South.[7] The next closest geographic concentration of women's lands is in the Northwest, sixteen entries in the latest *Shewolf's Directory.*

Most Lesbian land groups have avoided publicity, certainly not seeking the kind of national publicity that Brenda and Wanda Henson had when they were the target of hate crimes in Mississippi [see story, p. 142]. The Hensons' experience is every Lesbian land group's worst nightmare, explaining why these groups usually guard their privacy, sometimes even concealing their legal name in publications like *Lesbian Land* and *Shewolf's Directory.* There

---

6 *Maize: A Lesbian Country Magazine*, edited by Jae Haggard and "published, duplicated, and distributed at Outland," women's land in New Mexico, PO Box 130, Serafina, NM 87569. Publication of *Maize* has followed the editors. During the years that Lee Lanning was editor (1983–97, issues #2–55), LNR funded publication, and continues to maintain ties with *Maize*.

7 *Shewolf's Directory* (sixth edition) groups Southern lands in three regions: South Central USA (Alabama, Arkansas, Mississippi, Missouri), Central East USA (Kentucky, Tennessee, North Carolina, Virginia, West Virginia), and Southeast USA (Florida). She has no land groups from Georgia or South Carolina in any of the six editions. Shewolf includes some intentional communities that we do not include in our count because they are not all-women (Dancing Rabbit in Missouri, Earthaven in North Carolina, and Twin Oaks in Virginia).

are fewer land groups than there used to be; many of the listings in *Shewolf's Directory* end up being one Lesbian's or one couple's home, with some land and an expansive dream.

This special issue collects interviews and writings by Lesbians who lived (or are still living) in Lesbian land communities in Southern states. These are personal stories drawing on personal memories, all affected by the passage of time. Inevitably, there will be differences in the ways that community members experienced or remembered the same events. We have tried to include different perspectives when possible. We are archiving all of our interviews at the Sallie Bingham Center for Women's History and Culture in the David M. Rubenstein Rare Book & Manuscript Library at Duke University (http://library.duke.edu/rubenstein/bingham/). As with all the projects of the Southern Lesbian Feminist Activist Herstory Project, we intend to stimulate your memories and motivate you to record your own story of creating change and community.

Rose Norman, Merril Mushroom, and Kate Ellison
Fall 2015

OUR LANDS, OUR SELVES

Corky Culver

We drive hours through wickets of franchise signs
through gas fumes and fast foods and consumer chaos
finally, to a road where we grin to see
a handmade sign, "SNAKE CROSSING,"
we crunch up steep gravel drives before GPS
where patriarchy can't go
and TV cameras, thank the Lordess, haven't been.

Corky Culver, migrant farm working in Oregon in 1962. Her then girlfriend
Cathy Drompp (still a member of the North Forty) was traveling with her.
"We were traveling and stopping to pick at various farms to pay for our travels, on
the way back to Florida. They lent us extra clothes for a cold rainy day.
Other migrants gave us wood and milk."

On one land we find a mailbox shaped like a
flamingo painted pink and purple,
on another a rainbow of dancing daisies,
or a bed board with curlicue carvings, cunning codes,
hands clasped, or lips like flames,
spirals and seashells,
all spelling wimmin's land. Yes!

Photo by Rose Norman

Chicken coop at Sugarloaf Women's Village.

We cross a boundary
to where organic gardens and goddesses are,
where rosemary thrives and five kinds of basil,
where borage blossoms top salads,
and there are cutoffs and cutups—
and weeds and wild and winds
let us breathe.

Where each side of a cottage is a different color—
yellow, lavender, pink, and orange,
where the outdoor showers
are topped with statue of liberty mirrors
and beaded necklaces hang everywhere,
where a goofy ceramic frog
greets us beside the path. "Rivet!!"

Where a chicken coop sign announces
"LADIES ONLY"—no roosters here,
and where two hens eschew the
other open nests to
cuddle together in the same one,
and after they lay their eggs,
we hear them cackle and carry on.

Where tensions can be resolved by singing together
and hugging and circling
"if ever I have had a friend,
you've been a friend to me,"
and tensions sometimes
can be exacerbated by meetings without
singing and meditation.

Where folks can relax, where "in style"
means expressing one's mood of the moment
rag tag and dinner gowns
glitter and feed sacks,
and topless 42 D's swinging in the breeze,
where a splinter or a tick or a headache draws the attention
of five women's herbal remedies and coos of sympathy.

Where chainsaws notch the opposite side of the cut
women with lovely flushed faces lift logs end over end

for their fires and woodstoves.
Where women do their own carpentry and design
and go slow enough to show others,
measuring, sawing, drilling, painting, building houses,
building dreams.

Where a tree grows in the middle of a cabin,
where a cabin lives in the middle of a tree,
where a yurt is furnished with
a sleeping bag, antique canvas striped sling chairs,
garage sale finds, worn quilts,
a hot box stove
and a grandmother clock.

Where in the two hours when a generator
runs, all the batteries are charged, the
sewing machine runs and dance music charges the women,
where a newcomer apologizes for peeing in the composting toilet
and an old-timer says it's okay, it happens
where the hand pump builds muscles, elicits
a bouquet of cold water screams from a bevy of nudes.

Where deer gaze curiously at all
this human outdoor life, and hope the women
will forget to bring in the trays
of sunflower sprouts
leaving them outside all night for a deer nosh,
where love is made under the sky
and everyone feels warmed.

Where jars of spring water gather full moonlight
beside moon circles, lunar energy to be saved for boosts
during the month,
where drums sound, where campfires are sung to

clouds are sung to, maples and oaks are sung to,
growing vegetables are sung to
and many hear those vegetables singing right along with us.

Where women's art and rare books by women
are everywhere,
where few things are store-bought
and natural areas are left and weeds are welcome,
where constellations are given new names
("That one's Judy Grahn's suitcase!"
"There's Adrienne's Apple!").

Photo by Pat Paul, courtesy of Corky Culver

Corky Culver working in a neighbor's hayfield, 1975.

Where women are
making teapots and baskets and cutting leather shoes,
and knitting handspun yarns into scarves
and making rugs and hammocks on looms,
where a bandana on the door means
"In solitude for now, no visits please
see you later."

These lands are meccas where travelers come from around the world
and deep souls find each other.
As we chant and we plant, as we sing,
as the smoke rises and the sparks fly upward
and the steam rises off bodies in the
horse trough hot tubs, as the fog lifts

as earth and sky are joined
as we pray that the baggage
and wounds that we bring
do no harm and be healed,
we touch the earth and raise energy
on this hallowed ground, holy ground, these lands
that are home.

THE NORTH FORTY[1]: FLORIDA (1972—PRESENT)
by Kathleen "Corky" Culver

"Forty acres of oak trees dripping with Spanish moss; sandy clearings with pine needles sparkling in the sun; long time friends as neighbors." "Long Leaf," in *Lesbian Land* (1985), p. 83.

In 1969, Corky Culver and nine other members of a Lesbian conscious-raising group started by Judith Brown[2] in Gainesville, Florida, formed a group to look for land to start an intentional community for Lesbians. In 1972, they bought land they called The North Forty, near Melrose, Florida. It is possibly the first Lesbian land group in the country.

Part One: How We Did It

Some of you will want to get a land group going. Here's our story to encourage you.

How is it that we were the first women's land and that we have kept it going for forty-two years? Good question, says I to myself, knowing what a hard process it can be, how impossible it can seem.

Okay. First we were a consciousness-raising group, doing it in classic women's liberation style: speaking from our own experience, developing theory, doing action. We were, granted, getting the land for ourselves, but hoping to model a feminist process that would enable other women to do the same.

---

1 Corky Culver, writing as Circledance, describes the land as Long Leaf in Joyce Cheney's *Lesbian Land* (Minneapolis: Word Weavers, 1985), and later expanded that piece for publication in *off our backs* (May 1, 2003). That same issue includes several essays about Lesbian land, including Kate Ellison, "Lesbian Land: An Overview," *off our backs* (May 1, 2003): 39–41.

2 Co-author of the influential pamphlet "Toward a Female Liberation Movement," known as "The Florida Paper" (Boston: New England Free Press, 1968).

Why did we want to buy land together rather than separately? As a Lesbian group in the late 1960s, we were aware that depending on our families or men didn't offer us any social security, so we decided we could be one another's social security. Odd, maybe, to think of women in our twenties thinking ahead so far, but we wanted a place where we could grow old with supportive friends. We wanted the sense of safety and support we could give each other, living close in a community, ready to help take care of animals, to help if we got sick. We decided not to go into the arrangement as couples, which, over the long haul, might not work out. Each had her own share and house, even if couples developed. We wanted a beautiful place that could have our shared values of having some wildness around us as well as small gardens and small lawns. We wanted a sense of open land where we could walk to one another's houses without climbing fences, a parklike setting.

How could we afford this beautiful oak, pine, and cedar forest interspersed with meadows for gatherings?

Most of us did not have secure jobs as yet or large enough incomes to buy on our own. Two members put up the down payment and the rest of us paid only $15 a month for years. We each had equal ownership, no hierarchy. To protect the land as an intact piece, we didn't have separate deeds but had life estates with quitclaim deeds. Ten of us, as I remember, each for our lifetime, would have two acres personal space, each sharing communally the remaining twenty acres. With the life estate method, we couldn't put up our share as collateral to get bank loans, so our housing had to be resourceful—as in small travel trailers, hand-built frame houses, tents, according to what we could afford.

As time moved on, we were able to gather resources enough to build houses to code with all the amenities. Not like the early days when my outhouse was a hole with a frame seat over it and a view of the stars, my shower outdoors, my stove a thrift store find from a steamship (a fridge, a stove, and a sink in one quite compact

Photo by Pat Paul, courtesy of Corky Culver

Dore Rotundo standing on the platform of the house she designed, 1975. Dore, a current resident of the North 40, was one of the first women architects in Florida.

piece about the size of a big chair).

What kept us going? Paying the minimal fees and building board by board was possible with odd jobs, modest jobs. And essential were the years of orderly meetings, careful paperwork, lots of music. Our day jobs were often part-time and rural. Some were teachers, techs, house painters, architects, artists, nurses. In the early days, we planted trees, picked oranges, painted houses, managed gas stations, clerked natural food stores, raked hay, did part-time newspaper work as stringers.

Four of the original ten remain, with four new members. Some members peeled off, often finding the meetings and the challenges of getting along with others, making decisions with others, too stressful.

To help us, other land groups shared their bylaws. The local women's community helped clear land and build. A lot of women and spirit went into it.

Lawyer friends helped with the complicated legal issues involved in cooperative ownership and keeping the land intact. We had in our membership a contractor and architect who guided the buildings and helped a lot. Women starting now could check with Lesbian Natural Resources for advice (see story p. 173).

Dear sisters, we encourage you to find a piece of land and leap in. The early days are rich with compensations for the tough conditions. You've got camaraderie to compensate for shortages of money and amenities. You've got physically invigorating work that's visionary and significant. It's fabulous working outside with friends. You're on the cutting edge. It feels great. Good luck!!!

Part Two: Thirtieth Anniversary on the Land—"Paradise: A Work in Progress"

A bright clear day. Dea, upon arriving at the North Forty, bounds across the meadow in her long skirt and sandals headed toward Pat and me where we are setting up an outhouse for a gathering. We have a homemade box with a toilet seat over a hole, and for privacy, sheets wrapped around trees. We are singing, harmonizing on Holly Near's "Mountain Song." Dea is smiling like a beautiful piece of cantaloupe. "This is it—a clearing in the woods, pine trees, oaks sparkling in the sunlight, women singing my favorite kind of music. I arrived, thought this is great, women's land. I heard you singing, and I thought this is paradise."

It's where it's safe to work outside topless, bottomless, where there's no need of fences, where the individual house sites melt into communal land, where there's no need of marking boundaries, where you can walk on sand paths to the nearby houses, each nestled in a woods patch and almost out of sight of each other.

There's nothing like the feeling of stepping onto a piece of women's land, stepping out of traffic and ads and real estate signs. Each woman knows it's hers in some way, reflects her. Because women's land is about all women, not just particular owners.

We often have a special kind of harmony that feels like singing.

But paradise? Not quite yet. We're working on it. But it's work.

Let's take just one issue. Pets. One of the first irritants that lets you know there's something awry in paradise.

Let's take a hypothetical:

There's the grasshoppers that Ellen thinks of as pets, eating Star's pet spider lily.

There's Alice's best four-legged friend Bruno chasing Sally's Siamese.

Greta decides to feed River's shepherd the meat the dog's been missing on the tofu diet River gives her.

River, meanwhile, removes the ant spray and roach spray from Ruth's cupboard when Ruth is away.

Ruth has gone to get her dog neutered, which incidentally, River thinks is fiendishly unnatural.

Madge adopts stray cats by the dozens. Songbirds on the land thin out.

Mary Tom's dog drags used tampons around the land, pulling them from trees where Timber has hung them to keep deer from her garden.

Maia doesn't believe in tampons but wrings out her sponges into a dish for Tinker to pour around her garden.

A parrot squawking speaks for all of us. Awk!

Back to the present moment: Shall we tell Dea or anyone on this day celebrating our being here thirty years, of the Canker under the rose, the worm under the cantankerousness? Shall we rain on the parade of their delicious sensations and idealism?

No. Of course not. But one thing must be cleared up.

"Dea, you didn't bring a dog, did you?"

Women working on the first house to be constructed on the North 40, which became Corky's home, 1975.

Photo by Pat Paul, courtesy of Corky Culver

Part Three: Forty-Two Years on the North Forty
how it was birthed by children being cast out
by their families, shunned or shamed as Lesbian
betrayers of their society's, family's plans for them,
refusing to carry the family honor and name,
how they found peers among the others cast out,
how they loved them and gloried in them and created
communities and revolutions and buildings and vegetable plots

how they sought a new place in the country
where they could honor the wild the unconventional
the weeds and works of the hands, where they
could shun the ways of the industrial, the commercial,
make their own music, make clothing of the imagination,
costumes of whimsy and difference

how by sharing they made few monies stretch to the many
wise to how little they needed of what others valued
how they learned the ways of their spot of earth, learned the names
of the sparkleberries, the nettles and blazing stars, how they let
nature stay near them, remembering to share with the deer
and deer moss, there before them

how they learned to build for themselves, use hammers and
chainsaws, squares and levels, how they scavenged and saved
how they pumped water and showered outside and watched
the path of the moon. how they were lovingly careful,
maintained roads and houses and paid taxes and kept records
and sang and played flutes and cherished seeing each other
and working together.

how they made each other happy and made each other miserable
how some left and some stayed. how they tried something very
hard, very revolutionary. how in many ways they succeeded.

DRAGON

Dolphin Dragon

When, at age thirty-seven, I landed at Dragon on May Day 1980, a birthday party for a six-year-old girl was in progress, and I was fairly delighted and amazed by my first taste of Lesbian community. Wimmin's land. My firsthand report only begins then.

For years, I had unhappy feelings about being cast into the role of "Southern" woman. I was only introduced to the concept of "lady" in junior high school, by my best friend, who thought it an admirable ideal. So I gave it a small chance. It was not for me, but there seemed to be future benefits in store for those who were able to so consciously mold themselves, sort of like feet . . .

I'm from West Texas, not East Texas, or South Texas, or the Hill Country. But such fine distinctions were lost on those (who I thought of as) Yankees of Chicago! After thirteen years in the Midwest and expanding my sense of geography, I did not think of Missouri as the South.

St. Louis was the Midwest, right? Therefore, all of Missouri was the Midwest?

I had not expanded my sense of personal geography (or history) enough to know that (1) Missouri was a "divided" state during the Civil War, though a "legal" slave-holding state, and (2) that the Ozarks, where I bought thirty acres, is its own entity, a sort of crypto-libertarian culture, and a Confederate guerrilla hideout zone. All this splittedness, I reflected by deliberately regaining (after a stint in New York) my accent and maintaining it deliberately—partly as a confounding stereotypes ploy, or so I thought.

In thinking of us as Southern wimmin's land, the first questions that pop into my head are about race, hard questions: How many wimmin of color (WOC) live or have lived here? Visited? What's the attitude of the "locals"? What color are the locals?

Difficult questions, maybe ones we don't like the answers to.

We could not be said to encourage visitors—except our friends, of course, and mostly those from other women's lands, where we visited and romanced back and forth. Of course. But the tourism model of wimmin's land did not appeal to us, particularly to some of us: "We are not on exhibit. Don't come parading your city friends through here. We are not a theme park. This is where we live. This is our home."

I think that with the return of the First Wave,[1] the general outreach to visitors was ditched in favor of more personal and informal happenings. Such was the equally informal sense of the group. We also ditched meetings, electing to proceed haphazardly and guided by omens and mood.

Visitors, of course, did show up. Usually, the ones who just suddenly appeared did pretty well on the land. Many of those who wrote and sent resume-type letters and who we wrote back to— simply never appeared. Most.

The WOC who did visit Dragon were invited, either by us or by someone who knew us and was coming to be On The Land.

When Midwest Wimmin's Festival (MWF) was in Full Swing (it's in Small Swing now), there was a regular path running between the city wimmin and the country dykes. We met regularly for planning meetings, a whole series in Columbia that I recall, and later a round in Northern Arkansas. City wimmin meant some WOC, and there was one WOC who was a regular and longtime part of the planning meetings. More joyously, there were several years (the last years before the state park put the screws on?) when there were good numbers of various colors, classes, and abilities.

We made it our priority to be aware of class, disability, and racism—or the lack thereof—recognizing them as inherited and unnecessary barriers to our sisterhood, or peace and community. Seldom was the reality as one would hope, though

---

1 First Wave: Idiosyncratic usage for the return of four of the women who were not Original Dragons, and who all left and then returned five years later.

MWF did a commendable job, and we at Dragon mostly bumbled around. Other lands were more accessible than we were.

That presence of wimmin and kids of color at MWF probably felt more like progress than anything else we Ozark dykes did, as far as my sense of moving forward on a gaping gap in our shaping of a future worth living in.

We were also regularly exposed to (and sometimes participated in) the intrepid Susan Wiseheart's *Practicing Anti-Racism* (*PA-R*) newsletter. It is hard to gauge the effects of something like a small publication circulated among a small number of wimmin, but personally, I felt heartened with each new issue, proud to see our local town on the return address, and to learn the names of others doing this work, what they were doing, what their experiences were, and what suggestions they had for interrupting racism. It was important to us to receive and circulate *PA-R* ourselves, and we also were greatly encouraged by the contact with like minds that it gave us: a network before there was online networking, of course. Wimmin know how to do this in our bones.

In 1984, Athena Peanut, Kymara Badger, and Dolphin journey to Crystal Mountain in Arkansas and shoot a short super-8 movie protesting mechanized crystal mining there. This was a Dragon-sponsored event in that it would never have happened if our entire Ozarks feminist culture had not existed—and that culture was all-female, not all-Lesbian.

When I came, there was a tradition of the area women getting together for a New Moon celebration/potluck. The het (can't call 'em straight, sez Isis) women were mostly hippie immigrants, though there were also born and bred locals, who were fun, good cooks, smart, unique—just like all the rest of us. There was a women's softball team, sponsored by our beloved very local health food store. Our kids were friends with their kids.

Dragon does not exist as an island. Several womyn's lands are nearby. Greentree adjoins us. The Mound adjoins Greentree, and on the other side of our wide wooded county is Hawk Hill and a host of smaller lands, occupied by single Lesbians and couples, as well as a gay men's campground.

Since Dragon was included in *Lesbian Land* in 1985,[2] we have managed to burn down the Main House, pay off the pump, let the fields grow over, build a house, haul in two ready-mades, watch the garage fall down, grow food, make wine, bury one Lesbian, lose several, gain new ones, receive kind donations and moral support, and appreciate our good fortune in living here.

Now here we are: shitting in buckets of sawdust, carrying jugs of water, and warming ourselves with wood fires, none of this with quite the agility or speed as when we began.

What next? We die. Other ones come along and carry on. Hopefully. The land remains.

---

2   Edited by Joyce Cheney (Minneapolis: Word Weavers Press).

LANDYKE IN A STRANGE LAND, RURAL MIDDLE TENNESSEE
BELLY ACRES, 1975–PRESENT

Merril Mushroom

The 1960s was an exciting time to be in New York City. I was a twenty-something transplanted Southern bar dyke turned hippie dyke living in the East Village. I worked as a schoolteacher in central Harlem and otherwise was involved with civil rights, antiwar/peace activities, psychedelics, and Lesbians. My social group was the only predominantly gay/Lesbian group in psychedelia.[1]

In 1966, I opened a hippie shop in the East Village with another Lesbian and a gay man. We sold handmade crafts and worked with runaways, street kids, and antiwar protesters. We cooked and served free hot supper every evening to anyone off the street who wanted to eat—stews made from grains and beans bought with cash donations and free vegetables gleaned from the produce stands that lined First Avenue. The first Peace March happened, and the first Be-In at Sheep's Meadow in Central Park. I went to Millbrook and to Woodstock, danced at the Balloon Farm which later became The Electric Circus, and was involved with the Off-Off-Broadway theater scene. I ate peanuts at The Ninth Circle, eggs Benedict at the Limelight, steamed clams at the Riviera, pastelitos from the Argentine empanada stand next to The Hip Bagel, and macrobiotics at the Cauldron. I went to concerts at Fillmore East and hung out at the Caffe Cino, the Sea Colony, Kookie's, and the Washington Square.

---

1   See "The Illicit LSD Group—Some Preliminary Observations" by Frances E. Cheek, Stephens Newell, and Mary Sarett in *Psychedelics,* ed. Bernard Aaronson and Humphrey Osmond (New York: Doubleday & Co., Inc, 1970). Online at http://www.drugtext.org/The-Psychedelics/the-illicit-lsd-group-some-preliminary-observations.html.

The next wave of feminism was approaching. I quit teaching and went to work for a motorcycle courier service as their first woman delivery rider, and I drove a taxi for a while, but not at night. There were riots at the Stonewall bar, and Women's Liberation was blossoming. We dykes tore our shirts off and danced topless, liberated, breasts to breasts, in the Lesbian clubs.

As the psychedelic 1960s began to wane, and the hippie movement became a market, some of my friends drifted into the urban corporate establishment. Others moved from The City to rural areas as part of the simpler-living, back-to-the-land, renewed intentional community movement. This idea interested me, especially in the context of working with children. I shared a communal house in Tivoli, across the road from the Catholic Worker Farm, and even though I did not live there full time, communal living appealed to me. By 1970, I was increasingly drawn to the idea of collective country living and had a growing desire to raise and teach children outside the mainstream models of family and school. My inspiration was Aldous Huxley's book *Island*. One of my head shop partners was a radical fairie I had known since the 1950s in Florida. We discussed at great length the possibility of forming a partnership where we would adopt children who were "hard-to-place" (which was any child other than a healthy white baby), leave the city, and engage in rural communal living and collective free school. We would legally marry, if necessary, to be able to adopt; but I was a Lesbian, and he was a gay man, and we had no intention of giving up our same-sex girlfriends and boyfriends or our Lesbian and gay activities.

In 1972, we departed from New York City in a big pink school bus outfitted for living with our rescued street dog and our first adopted child—a biracial foundling boy—in search of the gay hippie pie-in-the-sky paradise that awaited us in, we thought, New Mexico, where several of our New York friends had gone to live at the Hog Farm.

We traveled for over a year and covered 15,000 miles around the United States, Canada, and Mexico. Despite our plans to settle in the West, we just did not feel at home anywhere we went. We longed for our familiar Southeast where we both had grown up, even though this was the very area we'd agreed that we should avoid as the white parents of a Black child.

But the Southeast of the 1970s was not the Southeast we remembered from the 1950s and 1960s, and tensions around race relations, although decidedly present, were not what they had been, either. Julia, in Georgia, who decided to join us in the collective, urged us to consider North Georgia, Tennessee, or Kentucky.

Meanwhile, we had run out of money and needed to get back to working at real jobs in order to be able to eat and buy gasoline while we looked for land. We decided to stop and settle temporarily in Knoxville, because it was conveniently located, and, most important, we were connected with the Knoxville Lesbian Feminist Alliance (KLFA). Friends from afar began to contact us to commit to the potential land collective.

Lesbian-feminist activity was burgeoning throughout the Southeast (see *Sinister Wisdom* issue 93). Many of my friends were becoming separatists, and I agreed wholeheartedly with them in theory—but in real life, here I was in a living arrangement with all these males!

The land search was continuing. Then, one day, we read in an old magazine a letter from a pair of vegetarian counterculture folks who had settled in rural Middle Tennessee where land was cheap and the locals were friendly, and they invited "like-minded folks" to come check out the area. We decided that could be code for us.

We went to visit. She was chopping the wood while he made and served the tea. We liked them. They took us to see a hill farm for sale nearby, on a hundred acres of extremely rough but very beautiful land, with two fixable houses, two usable barns, water on the land, in the perfect location, at an amazingly low price. We contacted potential collective members and pooled our money for the down payment. In 1975, we purchased the land and named it Belly Acres.

Our initial land group could not have been a more unlikely collection of folks. The core members were myself plus radical fairie co-parent plus, by now, two very young adopted boy children, two radical Lesbian-separatists, and a heterosexual man. Several people from our old New York group came to visit, interested in joining us as well. We thought that with a large enough piece of land and separate living spaces, we could work out or, at least, bypass our sociopolitical differences.

Our first projects were cleaning the two old houses, making them marginally livable, building a proper outhouse, and creating a womyn-only space. Living on the land was demanding. We had electricity but no running water. We cooked with gas, heated with wood, and washed our clothes in the laundromat up in town ten miles away. We kept chickens, ducks, turkeys, peafowl, dogs, cats, one horse, and many children.

That same letter that attracted us also brought to the area many other kinds of counterculture folks from other places, but there were almost no other gay/Lesbian people. (That, since, has changed, and the area now is home to a tremendous GLBTQ population.) We formed our free school, which took root and persisted for almost a decade. Three more children joined the family, but the other members of the collective dropped out during the first few years. The sociopolitical differences, it seemed, did matter; but these turned out to be not the greatest of our disagreements. Much more difficult to get past were the day-to-day issues around work that did or did not get done.

Work Ethic: 1975
This afternoon, when I arrived back home from my job in the city, and I saw you
sitting on the porch wearing brand-new overalls—

both of you sitting
on the porch with the two of them, your houseguests,
all of you wearing brand-new overalls—
and yes, I could imagine how you might have said,
in the car on your way to town,
"We'll need to buy some overalls to wear
when we work."
I wondered,
then,
did you really intend to use those overalls properly,
or did you think it would be sufficient just to know how to
fasten the galluses?

I see
firewood not stacked, not even split yet,
compost overflowing the bucket,
water jugs still empty,
dirty dishes piled on the counter,
chickens not yet fed,
eggs not collected,
no supper on the stove,
and
the four of you sitting on the porch
wearing your nice, clean, brand-new
overalls.

Lordesses, forgive me for being pissed off. Help me
not to be so judgmental,
to hold my tongue—to understand that
people have different ideas regarding
the day-to-day priorities
of collective country living.
But hay must not stay on the ground
when the weather threatens rain!

One of my jobs was as a breadwinner in the real world, to earn the money to pay the mortgage and other bills. As folks dropped out of the collective, those who remained had to pick up the farm debt. Finally, it was just me working away from the land, and my little paycheck stretched and stretched. We grew what food we could, but our garden was rough and rocky, and the ground needed lots of organic buildup to even begin to resemble soil. We traded with our neighbors, shopped at bale stores and salvage yards, tore down old buildings in exchange for the building materials. We participated in buying clubs, work parties, and clothing exchanges, went to barn dances, and played lots of music together. We did community organizing among the locals and got along well with our neighbors.

Most of the new folks settling into the area were heterosexual hippies, breeders, and there were many, many children who all flowed in and out among households. One might think that living among all these heterosexuals—hippie or not—that I had to be lonely for Lesbians, but, truth be told, I had plenty of dykes in my joyfully nonmonogamous life. Indeed, I could not have survived without them. Friends, lovers, or just passing through, Lesbians came to visit, and I went to them, to where they lived, to conferences, festivals, networking meetings. Whenever I was not working at my paycheck job, raising the children, doing house and garden chores, hauling water, writing stories, or doing rural community activism, I was somewhere doing something with the Lesbians!

Looking back on then from now, I can't believe I squeezed so much activity into every day and still got enough sleep. Our child population continued to increase. There were foster children, "stray" kids whose moms were not able to care for them right then, and sometimes the moms stayed with us, too. Our by now five adopted children grew up with the understanding that families come in many different arrangements and configurations, that Lesbian/gay orientation is just a regular way for some people to be, and that feminist values and practices were what we should aspire for in life.

Photo courtesy of Merril Mushroom

Wholesome, organic children raised at Belly Acres (l to r): Scott, Ananda (top), J'aime, David, Jessie (front).

By the early 1980s, I was working several paycheck jobs and had little time for anything else except children, garden, and Lesbians. I was in a monogamous relationship with a Lesbian who lived nearby. The free school had evolved into several smaller homeschooling groups. Radical fairies began to move to the formerly anarchist collective on Short Mountain, heralding the beginning of the GLBTQ population explosion in the area; and the Landykes movement was taking root in the Southeast as it was everywhere there were Lesbians.

ARKANSAS LAND AND THE LEGACY OF SASSAFRAS

Merril Mushroom

From interviews with Diana Rivers and Brae Hodgkin[1]

In 1972, Diana Rivers, an artist and political activist from Stony Point, New York, moved to Arkansas with her then boyfriend. Land in Arkansas was inexpensive, remote, unspoiled, and beautiful. The towns of Fayetteville and Eureka Springs drew young people who were involved in the back-to-the-land, counterculture, hippie movements of the 1970s. Diana bought 500 acres of land in Newton County and established a primarily heterosexual community of women and men called Sassafras. The land was mountainous and rugged, had no electricity or running water, and the driveway was over a mile long.

Over the next few years, the wave of feminism washed into Northwest Arkansas, and the women at Sassafras became increasingly angry as they became better informed about the oppression of women. Growing dissatisfied with their restrictive relationships with men, they began turning to each other for love and support. They became feminist, then Lesbian, then separatist. Many of the women no longer wanted to live with men.

Due to the death of her son, Diana had to leave for a while. When she returned, she was summoned to a meeting by the women of the land. They wanted Sassafras to become a women's land, and they wanted her help in making it happen. In spite of still being in pain from her son's death, she agreed to their plan with some reservations. Soon a meeting at Sassafras was called

---

1   Rose Norman interviewed Diana Rivers at Womonwrites on May 24, 2012. Rose Norman interviewed Brae Hodgkin at Womonwrites on October 15, 2011, and May 24, 2014.

in which the women informed the men still living there that they wanted the men to vacate and the land to become a women's land community. It was a harsh, contentious meeting that went on all day, with women's anger erupting frequently. Diana kept hoping the community would work it out among themselves, but in the end, she had to decide because the land was still in her name. (Earlier, the Sassafras community had tried unsuccessfully to get the land into a land trust.) Diana was quite a bit older than the others, so this was not her first turn at politics. Several times, she tried in vain to warn women, "Be careful! How you treat the men today is how you'll treat each other tomorrow." Unfortunately, this turned out to be all too true.

Men left and women took over the land. The only exception was that the land above the bluffs was deeded to a young couple whom the women regarded as working class and therefore worthy. Women settled into two collectives, the Blue Creek Tribe based in and around the main house (the original old farm house) and Lesperadoes living in a hippie-built house lower down on the land.

Diana went to Oregon with her girlfriend and was gone for more than a month. By the time she came back, the two collectives were at war with each other, and both complained angrily to her about the other, trying to enlist her help. It got so bad that when women from the Ozark Women's Land Trust heard about it, they left their meeting, got in their trucks and cars, and drove down from Missouri to mediate a settlement, saying that, "This kind of behavior threatens women's land everywhere and won't be tolerated." An uneasy truce ensued, and by the next week, they were all planning a Thanksgiving dinner together.

Meanwhile, in 1975, Brae Hodgkin and her girlfriend Brodie moved to Leslie, Arkansas, and later were joined by their friends Dusty and Aurelia, another couple. The land near Leslie was a forty-acre parcel purchased by an older couple named Cappy and Joan, who had met in divorce court in State Farm, Pennsylvania, and moved to the dyke community in Tucson. The Arkansas land was to be their retirement farm. They named it Elggurts, "struggle" spelled backwards, saying "we struggle backwards." They invited other Lesbians from the Tucson community to move to the land and build houses.

As dykes are known to do, Aurelia and Brodie got together, while Brae and Dusty, drowning in their tears, determined to get out of town fast. They decided to hitchhike together to the Michigan Festival, even though they had no camping gear. Shortly before leaving for MichFest, Brae saw a notice about Sassafras posted at a hippie co-op store in Leslie, announcing the formation of a women-only collective. When they got to Michigan, Brae met women from Blue Creek Tribe who invited her to come live at Sassafras. She took up residence in the pottery shed near the main house.

Sassafras was described as "open women's land," which meant that all women were welcome there. They could just show up and be part of it. The idea of open women's land evolved from women in the hippie movement becoming radicalized and realizing that there was more to life than raising children and working in the kitchen. It was an old story that on the hippie communes, men worked in the fields and stayed outdoors while women were relegated to the kitchen and waited on the men when they came in. Many women were dissatisfied with this arrangement, and their new feminist ideas empowered them to make changes. The idea of separatism was a logical extension, as the pendulum had to swing to the other side before it could come back to the middle again. Open women's land also provided a resting place for traveling Lesbians who needed space where they could feel welcome, as early hippie communes often could be quite lesbophobic.

The women's community in the town of Fayetteville was very well organized, and the women in town were supportive of the women at Sassafras. There was the Ozark Women's Trucking Collective, a food co-op, a children's house where children of Lesbians could stay, and many women in the community owned or rented houses that were open for women to reside. There was a women's gym, a women's café, and an active political community. Women set up alternative commerce connections in order to do business only with women. In typical Lesbian fashion, many, many meetings took place around issues having to do with racism, classism, spirituality, and cooperative collective structure. There also were a few "open land" communities in Missouri nearby, and residents of Sassafras often interacted with Lesbian women from Dragon in Ava, Missouri, which they considered their sister community (see pp. 25, 108 and 130 for Missouri women's land stories).

Toward the end of the 1970s, things began to fall apart. There was a great deal of friction around issues of sexuality, race, and class, both on the land and in town, where women were trying to create a "wimmin-centric" economy. There were struggles around political correctness, with hours of processing, and disputes regarding the supposed alternative commerce method.

Brae was part of the women's trucking collective, which worked well for a while, until some of the Lesbians went back to being straight and wanted to let men be part of the trucking collective. She sees this time as a steep learning curve, "creating our dyke culture—albeit doing it on steroids, so to speak." The women talked a lot about anger and allowing women to be angry without being stigmatized. Brae observed that "there were many women in the community from diverse backgrounds and life experiences, some of whom were just beginning to learn their voice and express it in an environment where they were suddenly welcomed or not."

When the Lesbian separatists tried to deal with issues, matters got even worse. It seemed that as long as it was "us against them," Lesbians could maintain a united front, but when there were divisions from within, according to Diana, there were "lots of horrific meetings" with women, suddenly empowered, expressing anger based on oppression but twisted by personal shortcomings, leading to manipulation, accusations, guilt, and blaming rather than behaving like feminists. As the primary landowner, Diana became the target for much of the anger. She saw the situation at Sassafras continuing to deteriorate as they failed to find common ground around differences of politics, culture, ethnicity, and class. Arguments about residency and use of the land deteriorated in one case to the point of litigation in the local court.

By the late 1970s, only a few full-time residents remained at Sassafras, with most of the wimmin traveling to town for paycheck jobs. In an attempt to bring more wimmin back to the land full time, a crafts collective was formed by Brae, Diana, Honest, and Cedar, with the intention of pooling income from making and selling T-shirts, cards, candles, bronze and copper jewelry, and other craft items. The crafts collective was called Wild Magnolia. Tensions between the women at Sassafras continued to increase significantly.

There were no women of color on the land at that time, and Caucasian women were guilt-ridden over this fact, so they went seeking women of color from the area. In 1979,[2] a portion of the land was deeded to a group identifying as working-class women of color. They called it Rainbow Land, established a board of directors, and formed a corporation, Arco Iris, Inc. [see p. 43 Arco Iris]. The political situation continued to worsen at Sassafras, until tensions became overwhelming, and finally the Wild Magnolia women left the land.[3] In 2000, after the land had been abandoned

---

2 The women of color actually moved onto the land in about 1977, and the land was deeded to them in 1979. The year 1979 comes from the online *Encyclopedia of Arkansas History and Culture,* "Women's Intentional Communities aka: Women's Land Communities," http://www.encyclopediaofarkansas.net/encyclopedia/entry-detail.aspx?entryID=6513, which says that before 1979, "For a short time, the women's land was operated by two collectives, the Blue Creek Tribe and the Lesperados."

3 At the end of her self-published book about her time on womyn of color land in Northern California, *The La Luz Journal* (1980), Juana Maria Paz describes moving to Fayetteville, Arkansas, in the fall of 1979, when "the collective [at Sassafras] had just split up" (78). She describes the time she spent living at Rainbow Land (now Rancho Arco Iris) that winter: "My tribal fantasies were fueled by the existence of another womyn-of-color land though I was heartily disappointed to find it empty." Residents were on a trip to Texas.

for some years, the two remaining members deeded 400 acres to the Arco Iris nonprofit corporation.[4]

In 1980, a number of women, including some who had left Sassafras, began meeting to discuss forming a new women's land community. The phoenix which rose from these ashes was called the Ozark Land Holding Association (OLHA). About twenty women purchased 240 acres near Fayetteville, and the community continues to this day.[5]

Stone wall inside Diana Rivers' house at OLHA. The stones for the wall and floor were carried by womyn's hands only, and set by Diana.

OLHA was and is "the legacy of Sassafras," and much of the working structure was developed as a result of the Sassafras

---

4 Shiner Cardozo and Diana Rivers were the only people whose names remained on the deed to the Sassafras land that had not been deeded to others. Diana and her life partner Path Walker retained a life estate in ten acres of the 400 acres deeded to Arco Iris.

5 Lee Lanning and Nett Hart interviewed OLHA women for *Lesbian Land* (ed. Joyce Cheney, 1985), where it is called "Maud's Land." Sassafras, Arco Iris, OLHA, and other women's lands in Arkansas are described in Allyn Lord and Anna M. Zajicek, "Women's Land Groups (early 1970s–2000)," in *The History of the Contemporary Grassroots Women's Movement in Northwest Arkansas, 1970–2000,* pp. 33–36. Fayetteville, AR: University of Arkansas Press, 2000. (75p).

experience, especially the use of contracts, which "keep it clear and clean." OLHA established bylaws and runs by a consensus-minus-one process. Decisions are based on "triangle of interest"— how any decision will affect the individual, the community, and the land. OLHA is considered Lesbian land but not separatist. Most of the women have men in their lives, but the presence of men is restricted and subjected to member approval[6]. Housing and accommodations have evolved as members age and their needs change. Some live on the land, some have a space on the land but live elsewhere, and some live in town (Fayetteville). OLHA currently has about fifteen members. Membership cost is based on each woman's share of the land payment. New members must be approved by the current members and can buy in only if another member wants to sell.

Diana is a resident at OLHA, while Brae lives on the North Forty, Lesbian land in North Central Florida [see story, p. 19].

---

6 Groups define separatism in different ways. Some Landykes would consider the OLHA policy "separatist." Some groups who are regarded by others as separatist, do not regard themselves as separatist.

ARCO IRIS, RAINBOW LAND:
THE VISION OF MARIA CHRISTINA MOROLES
Águila

Maria Christina Moroles (b. 1953), known as Sun Hawk, recently graduated to Águila (Eagle). Águila founded and has lived on the beautiful, rugged, mountainous land that is called Rancho Arco Iris for nearly forty years. In October 2014, she told her story to Rose Norman, who helped condense that long interview for this special issue.

In the Beginning

I came to this mountain because of a vision that began as a recurring dream that started when I was just a teenager. Several tragedies occurred during my teens: I was raped when I was twelve years old, and gave birth when I was thirteen. I gave the baby up for adoption. Also at age 13, I was brutally beaten, and I witnessed a friend's murder. When I was around seventeen, I again became pregnant after being raped, and my brother was murdered. The dream started while I was living on the streets of Dallas after being estranged from my traditional Mexican Indian family, who lived in a barrio there. The dream would often wake me, and at first, it was very frightening. In this dream, I was on a mountaintop, standing alone, looking down into a valley. The valley was like a city, but the city was in a war; I could hear shooting, bombs exploding, and people crying out. It was a terrible scene, and I felt saddened by it, but I felt safe where I stood.

I began to dream of leaving the city and finding that mountain. When I was about nineteen, I hitchhiked to Austin, and hung out on Guadalupe Street, where there was a big street fair. It rained all weekend, and I got pretty sick. A young couple, who frequently took sandwiches to the homeless, took me in. It was they who told me about this incredibly beautiful mountain: "There's a community that lives way back in the mountains. You don't have to pay anything to live there. We're going to move there."

That land turned out to be Sassafras, about 500 rugged, mountainous acres near Fayetteville, Arkansas. It was a hippie commune at that time, but later, it was claimed as Lesbian land. [See "Arkansas Land and the Legacy of Sassafras," p. 36]. I began to save money and to prepare myself and my family to leave the city and find my safe dream mountain. The dream continued, and I knew that this land must be where I should go.

Moving to Arkansas

We moved to Fayetteville in 1973, when my daughter was two. Sassafras was an hour and a half away. The first time I drove up to that mountain, my heart opened; I knew I was home. I had never seen anything more beautiful than that beautiful dirt road, lined with every kind of hardwood tree. I was in love! Unfortunately, the Sassafras community reminded me too much of the chaos that I had left behind in Dallas—they had just brought it out into the woods. There was an abundance of drugs and alcohol, and people playing Indians and witches, trying on all kinds of different hats. I was not interested one iota in that, and I went back to Fayetteville to cry about it.

About two years later, I got into a relationship with a woman, a dear friend, Patti Cardozo, known as Shiner. She was a member of the collective that owned Sassafras, and she told me the land had changed—it was women's land now. Again, my heart opened, and I thought I would try again. Shiner wasn't on the land when we went out. Another friend, Esther Martinez, who was staying with us, went with me. We were greeted at the gate by a couple of very hostile Lesbian women who asked who we were and what we wanted. I told them we were friends of Shiner Cardozo, and that she had invited us to come there. They said, "Well, she's not here." Once again, I saw that the land was not welcoming me. But then Berry, a young nurse from Germany, came up to me and said, "I was here when you came the first time, and I saw you leave heartbroken. Now I see you again, and I believe you *do* belong here." We talked, and I told her my concerns and my sadness. She told me that there was land on the other side of the creek from Sassafras, land that belonged to Sassafras, and maybe we could live there, away from this community. She told me how to get there, and we decided to take that walk. It was a long journey, and I had a four-year-old with me, but I was determined. Arriving at the other side, I felt my heart opening again. Maybe this *was* the place. There was nothing there, but there was peace. I left with a possibility of what we could do.

My Death and Rebirth

Back in Fayetteville, an epidemic of contagious hepatitis was sweeping through our community like wildfire. Every woman in the trucking[1] community got it, including me. I begged Shiner not to take me to Sassafras for healing, but she came home one day to find me passed out on the floor, burning with fever, leaving me no choice in the matter. When I woke up, I found myself in the main house at Sassafras, where Berry was caring for me. The women of Sassafras, thinking I was dying, were drumming and chanting outside the building. Indeed, although Berry provided the best care she could, the illness overcame me, and I died. Berry went outside to tell the women I was dead, and they began crying and wailing. Then she went back in the building and sat alone with my body. While mourning over me, she said that all of a sudden I took a deep breath, and a white light shone all around my body.

During my death, I had a profound vision. I was told by a saintly looking young Indian woman with braids, a woman that I named Santa Maria, that I wasn't going to die, I was just resting. When I awoke, I was to start my life anew. She gave me my life's purpose,

1 Ozark Women's Trucking Collective was an all-Lesbian trucking collective for Ozark Food Coop Warehouse, based in Fayetteville. Maria, Shiner, and many Sassafras women drove long-haul trucks for it as far west as New Mexico, as far east as Alabama, as far south as New Orleans, and as far north as Wisconsin (picking up cheese).

my mission: this land was to be a sanctuary, a safe space, for women and children of color. While this is an abbreviated version of the vision it actually continued for several days. I remember being in a blissful state, where I wasn't in pain anymore. I felt good; I wanted to live.

After I regained some strength, I felt the urge to go outside. Berry dressed me in a beautiful white caftan that Shiner had left as a burial robe for me. There was snow on the ground, but it was a clear blue day, and everything looked so brilliant and beautiful to me. The yard looked over toward the mountain where I live now. It was cold, and I was barefoot, yet I felt very warm. Berry prepared a pallet for me outside, and I asked to be left alone. My vision continued, and I saw three Indians on horseback on the bluff across from me. The Indian in the center was waving to me with a staff, waving me to come. I looked into the sky, and there were buzzards flying around above me. Then out of the south a hawk came flying north, right down into the center of them, screeching loudly and scaring them away. The moment it flew above me and in front of the sun, I knew my medicine name: Sun Hawk. I had a new life, and that was my new name.

The Birth of Arco Iris

After I became well enough, I came over to Rainbow Land. At first, it was just my daughter, Jennifer, and me, but later, Esther Martinez came. Members of the Sassafras collective who had been there when I died and came back to life were so impacted by my vision that they decided to give me the 120-acre piece of land, which we later called Rancho Arco Iris. Although I don't believe in owning our Mother, I put the land in Esther and my names [2] in

2 According to the online *Encyclopedia of Arkansas History and Culture,* the land was deeded to Maria and Esther in 1979. See "Women's Intentional Communities aka: Women's Land Communities," http://www.encyclopediaofarkansas.net/encyclopedia/entry-detail.aspx?entryID=6513. Later, Esther's name was taken off and replaced by the woman who was then Maria's life partner and lived there twenty-eight years, leaving in 2011.

order for us to have autonomy and security in the knowledge that we would not ever be displaced.

The vision was that the land would be used to heal myself and to provide a sanctuary for women and children of color. At first many women came, women of color who had heard about us through different articles, word of mouth, and various events. We would attend the Michigan Womyn's Music Festival, where I would speak at a tent intended for women of color. Women were coming, and they were all wounded. We were all so wounded. It was crazy. We didn't have any money, and I was still recovering from hepatitis. We lived in tents and teepees with no running water, surviving on food stamps.

But then, more and more women began leaving—women who had had that dream of living on land, and escaping their traumas and tragedies and the madness of the city life. But they had tried it and found that it is not easy to live in a wilderness area. Sometimes women would leave their children behind, and I would take care of them, as I was already raising my little girl.

Back then, I had a little motorcycle that I would park at Sassafras. Jennifer, then only five years old, and I would hike in our supplies from one mountain, across a creek, and up our mountain. It would be about two years before we saved enough money to rebuild our road to drive in some times of the year. Rancho Arco Iris had virtually no road, no cleared land to speak of, no water, and, of course, no electricity. About a year later, I traded my motorcycle in for a little Ford pickup. Our three-mile-long road was a washed-out, old logging road that had hardly been used in decades. It had trees growing in it and ruts deep enough to lose a child in. We often had to walk in due to mud, snow, or ice. There were two one-room unfinished cabins on the land that we worked on so that women could stay in them. One has gone back to the earth. The other one is now Jennifer's cabin, which has been completely reconstructed.

Less than a year after moving onto the land, my partner, Shiner, who had left out of fear when she thought I was dying, returned. I told her the vision, and explained that the land was intended for community and as a sanctuary to share and hold sacred. Shiner supported my vision, and we began to work on it, as stewards.

After a while, Shiner's grandmother, who needed health care, came to live with us. We set Franny up in a small trailer, and my family lived nearby in a teepee. Her family paid us to be her caregivers and to provide for her needs. The income helped us build a house and upgrade our terrible dirt road.

Women built all the structures and orchestrated all the improvements that are here now. Over time, we rebuilt our road, and we installed a pond for fish, wildlife, irrigation, and recreation. My partner and I hand-dug and built a 900-gallon cement cistern tank into the ground next to our house to hold rainwater or springwater. Our first indoor water was a hand pump connected to the cistern. We used kerosene lamps and candles for most of thirty years and cooked all our meals over an outside fire pit for our first twenty-five years. We finally added solar electricity and got an antenna telephone when our son Mario was about four. There were no phone poles for three miles, and a pay phone was ten miles away. We hired well-drillers who drilled a 500-foot well that never worked because it requires a special water pump to run on solar power. So, instead, we developed a natural spring as our main source of water, which remains our main source of water to this day.

The Birth of Mario and a New Sense of Community

After several years of living with Shiner on the land, I met a woman in Michigan and invited her to come and help work on the house we were building. She was here about six months before we ended up falling in love. Mario, our son, was born in 1988. After his birth, we could no longer go to the festival in Michigan, as male children were to be separated from their mothers and placed in a camp. We had often taken care of little boys whose mothers brought them to the land; we had never been separatist in that way. And we weren't about to be separated from our son. Once we stopped going to Michigan, where we had informed other

Courtesy of Águila

Mario Solano, named after his bondmother, Maria Christina Moroles (Sun Hawk), in the cradle board she made for him, 1988.

women of our existence, the flow of women to the land lessened. But with Mario's birth, our lives changed, locally. He drew our community—this Bible Belt Christian community—together around us. Everyone was so drawn to him. All the white people, who would have never spoken to us before, somehow just fell in love with him. "He's a dandy!" they would say, adoring the fat little Indian baby in a cradle board. Everybody wanted to hold him and touch him and feed him. Of course, our boys grow up into men, so the shift in our community naturally progressed.

The Progression of Arco Iris

Sometime around 1984, we incorporated as a nonprofit survival camp for women and children of color. In about 1994, we gained 501(c)(3) status, and in 2000, we decided to ask for the land that had been the Sassafras community. For almost ten years, Sassafras had been mostly abandoned. Poachers were shooting the wildlife off season, digging up valuable roots, stealing and vandalizing the property, and just hanging out partying there. Those 400 acres are now owned by Arco Iris, and we call the 120 acres I live on Rancho Arco Iris, to differentiate.[3] Most recently, in 2014, we became land tax exempt.

An Inclusive Sanctuary

Arco Iris means rainbow in Spanish. Indigenous people believe the rainbow represents the rainbow goddess of healing. She is an aura of all colors, all the colors of all the peoples. Before we came here, long ago, this land was a healing place for all peoples to come. As an indigenous woman of North America, I know I was summoned here to this sacred land not only as a sanctuary for us survivors, but to protect this sacred mountain. As an indigenous daughter, I believed it is our inherent right and sacred responsibility to maintain the leadership and stewardship of this sacred place. Often my words have been misinterpreted as exclusive. Look around. How many native people do you see? There is your answer. I still look around and immediately miss my people that once inhabited all of North America. Will we allow ourselves to remember that many native and people of color are still disenfranchised and do not have equal privileges? My vision is to reserve space to include those less privileged that are seeking sanctuary, not to exclude anyone. I will never forget that this sacred land was returned to the hands of poor, indigenous, two-spirit women. It was placed in our trust, so that we could have sovereignty and autonomy, so that we could reclaim within ourselves our sacredness, our purpose, and our strength. I pray others who follow after me will understand our intention.

---

3   In the 1990s, they got LNR funding to purchase twenty or thirty adjacent acres with the spring they use for running water. This was added to the over a hundred acres deeded to Maria and Esther by the Sassafras collective in 1979. The 400 acres that had been Sassafras was deeded to Arco Iris by the two women who remained from the collective, Diana Rivers and Shiner Cardozo. Diana and her life partner Path Walker retain a life estate in about ten acres.

The Mission

Our mission today is still for all this land to be a sanctuary, not only for women and children of color, but for all people who come in peace and in search of sanctuary. It is an incredible, deep hardwood forest. Because of our remoteness, some areas were never logged. This land is full of elk, deer, bear, wild turkey, and wolves. We even have panthers. We have wild, rare, and medicinal herbs, and many edible mushrooms. There is so much medicine here—even the clay is healing. We are one of the most pristine areas in the Ozarks. For me, protecting this incredibly sacred land is a major, top-of-the-list item. If the land isn't protected, then those who come here are not protected.

We want to create a stewardship agreement to hold the land in perpetuity. I've written a draft that says that indigenous women will live on the land and work on it. The draft gives guidelines for how to care for these lands for future generations. It is a very complex thing that I've taken on as a sacred responsibility. Our mission now is to heal our community—our local community, our Ozark community, and our indigenous community—and to bring all the colors into sacred union again. I know that is quite ambitious, but these ancestors who called me back have been quite insistent. They knew exactly who they were dealing with, what kind of person would persevere, despite all the obstacles we have faced. It can be very hard for me as a nonacademic woman. I went to the seventh grade, and I got my GED by going to night school when I was very young. I do not have monetary or academic credentials that are often required in this society. But I do have perseverance and vision. I believe the ancestors called me back to protect this sacred land for all of us, and I pray that I will be able to do that.

Today

I have lived on this land for almost forty years now, and I have witnessed many changes. Currently, Mario lives with me here on the land, where we still live off the grid. At present, Mario and I are the only full-time resident stewards. He runs men's lodges for men, and I do women's lodges. Jennifer, my daughter, has a cabin here, but presently resides with her partner, Lisa, in a small town thirty miles away. My children, my family/community, and this sacred land are my life. We are in search of people, especially women with skills who can help us achieve our mission.

Giving Thanks

So many women over the years have helped build Rancho Arco Iris, but of all those women, I must especially acknowledge the woman who spent twenty-eight years with me at Arco Iris for all the years of love and care she put into both this land and into me. Her spiritual determination, her passion, her muscles, and her courage were a large part of making Arco Iris what it is today. A special thanks to all the indigenous elders who came here or sent prayers to bless us and support us. Thanks to Berry for nursing me to be here today, and to Juanita Arrega, Shiner, Marie Cavallo, Isis Brown, Marsha Gomez, Cynthia Perez, Celia Rodriquez, Eva Kulterman, Lucia Lopez, Shelby Wood, Tamara Collier, and Diana Rivers for protecting this land and supporting us and Arco Iris as we grow and change. We are also very appreciative of the many wonderful men who have worked with us, respected our ways, and been friends. Tlatzokamati to my children: Jennifer, who has weathered it all with incredible love, strength, and courage, and Mario, who is here today as my teacher, student, and steward to this land and me. Finally, I thank my partner Annais for helping me get this story ready for publication and for her love and trust over the past two years. Please forgive me if I did not put each of your names, as we have such a huge community, but know that you are in my heart of gratitude.

To learn more about land stewardship efforts at Arco Iris, see the Arco Iris Earth Care Project, http://earthcareproject.wordpress.com/

PAGODA, TEMPLE OF LOVE: LESBIAN PARADISE (1977—PRESENT)

Merril Mushroom

Every day there is a song, every night a gift of love,
every moon a celebration.
Inscribed on Pagoda letterhead

The Pagoda was not so much a community of dykes on the land as it was a community of dykes by the sea. Located on Vilano Beach, St. Augustine, Florida, it became a well-known "Lesbian paradise"[1] for women all over the South—indeed all over the world—and is an example of serendipity in action. It came about as the result of the vision of Rena Carney and Morgana MacVicar, Lesbian cousins, and their partners Cathy and Suzy. They had formed a women's theater and dance troupe called Terpsichore and performed throughout Florida. Their dream was to have their own theater. This dream was fulfilled beyond their wildest imaginings.

Pagoda was primarily an arts and spirituality-oriented community. In its "glory days" (about 1977–1999), Lesbian theater, dance, and music were performed in the fifty-seat Pagoda Playhouse. They also held workshops on every conceivable subject of interest to Lesbians. Through the years, many scores of Lesbians came through, stayed, visited, left, returned. The Pagoda Temple of Love was a center of women's spirituality and one of the first recognized goddess worshipping churches in the nation. Here we focus on the herstory and structure of this unique Lesbian-feminist community that has persisted for almost forty years, even through its many changes.

---

1 Nancy Unger, "The Pagoda: 'An Island of Lesbian Paradise,'" in *Queer Ecologies: Sex, Nature, Politics, Desire*, ed. Catriona Mortimer-Sandilands and Bruce Erickson (Bloomington: Indiana University Press, 2010), pp. 182–86.

This article has been synopsized from interviews with Morgana MacVicar, Fayann Schmidt, Barbara Lieu, Jean Adele, Ellen Spangler, Emily Greene, Myriam Fougère, and Rainbow Williams.[2] Barbara, Ellen, and Morgana were very active in the women's movement during the 1970s. They helped organize battered women's shelters, rape crisis centers, women's centers, antiwar protests, feminist theater, and many of the types of actions described in *Sinister Wisdom 93* (Summer 2014).

In 1977, Morgana, Rena, Cathy, and Suzy were living in St. Augustine and looking for the place that would be their theater. They saw an ad in the paper announcing "beachfront cottage for sale," and they went to check it out. The property had been built in 1936 as a motel and consisted of fourteen buildings. The owner actually wanted to sell four cottages, not one, and so the women scraped together all the money they could and bought them on 7/7/77.

The largest building on the premises was not for sale, but the women rented it to live in, and created their theater in the garage. Berkeley Women's Music Collective was the first band to perform there, in fall 1977. In April 1978, nine women bought four more cottages and the duplex (a total of six more units). They rented out some of the cottages they had purchased to dykes who came to visit. Some of the women lived in their cottages to run the "Lesbian resort" that opened for its first season in summer 1978.

Eventually, the Pagoda community came to include a total of twelve cottages plus a two-story duplex, a swimming pool, and

2 On April 14, 2013, Rose Norman interviewed as a group six Pagoda women now living at Alapine: Morgana McVicar, Fayann Schmidt, Barbara Lieu, Jean Adele, Ellen Spangler, and Emily Greene. On November 13, 2013, she interviewed Rainbow Williams at her home in St. Augustine, Florida. On January 28, 2014, she interviewed Myriam Fougère at her Pagoda cottage in St. Augustine. All quotations come from these interviews, except for Rainbow Williams, who (unless otherwise noted) is quoted from a manuscript originally published in *Maize*, in 2010, and subsequently updated in private correspondence with Rose Norman. The interviews in their entirety are archived at the Sallie Bingham Center for Women's History and Culture in the David M. Rubenstein Rare Book & Manuscript Library at Duke University (http://library.duke.edu/rubenstein/bingham/).

the Community Center/Temple of Love (the largest building). Meanwhile, all the women who were becoming involved with Pagoda got to work on what they were beginning.

Pagoda Motel postcard, showing layout of cottages on Vilano Beach, St. Augustine, in the 1970s. Since then, all of the surrounding lots have been developed.

At the end of summer 1978, problems began to arise. According to Barbara Lieu, "We've got ten units (eight cottages and a duplex) owned by thirteen women. It's not a collective, just women coming together financially. Those of us who were living here felt differently from those who were living elsewhere and just renting out the cottages to men or women. We felt strongly about permanently making it a women's space, and that was a conflict." The conflict happened when the male tenants were evicted. The women who owned the cottages all agreed that as male tenants left, Pagoda would become all-womyn space. However, there was disagreement as to the actual process, and some women felt that there was neither consensus nor discussion around the evictions.[3]

---

3 This interpretation of the conflict is based on an email from Vicki Wengrow to Rose Norman (September 27, 2014). Vicki owned one of the two cottages rented to men, and her partner Pat owned the other one.

In November, Emily and her partner Wiggy (later called Nu) came to visit and fell in love with the place. They overheard some of the women talking about selling and asked what was happening. They were told that there were two cottages for sale, and if Lesbians couldn't be found to buy them, they would be sold to men. Emily and Wiggy managed to raise the money for one of the cottages—$3000 down and $40–50 a month—and Karen Jones bought the other.

As time passed, cabins changed owners, and properties were bought and sold, but always to Lesbians. Throughout these processes, the women used the Consumer Price Index inflationary rate to keep the properties affordable for Lesbians. Women who worked on the property were paid, and everyone who worked on the premises, from lawyer to cottage cleaner, was paid the same rate, $5 per hour. Gradually, Pagoda became a residential community. In 1979, several women (maybe thirteen) gave enough money to make a down payment on the building that would become The Pagoda Temple of Love, which they incorporated as a church so that they could have tax-exempt status but still maintain women-only space.

The cottages were owned individually with verbal agreements to share services such as gas and water lines, septics, mortgages, and other infrastructure. Women participated in community activities—or not—to varying degrees, as they liked. According to Barbara, "We lived happily in a Lesbian environment, but there was no obligation to participate [in concerts, meetings, Temple activities], and no legal connection between the community building and the cottages. There was just an 'affinity connection.'" The community building was made into a "supporter" building where nonresidents could stay when they visited and, if they wished, be put on a list to buy a cottage if one became available.

Morgana and Barbara spoke about the psychic connection drawing people on a spiritual level to a place that had a life force of its own there already, that the women who were supposed to be there felt the call and came.

Ellen noted that "it was a safe place for Lesbians, and there weren't many places that was so, places where the whole spirit of women was really honored, spiritually, physically, emotionally. Everyone who was involved . . . was committed to making it work."

Photo courtesy of Emily Greene

Ellen Spangler doing carpentry inside Martha Strozier's Pagoda cottage. Ellen came down from Jacksonville the year that the first cottages were bought (1977) and helped create the theater and remodel many of the cottages.

Jean added, "When I look back and think about how it lasted so long, I think it was because we would get together and make decisions by consensus. Running that Center, we would have *long, long* meetings about how to do that. . . . We were very compatible, and we all got along and liked each other. What changed was when the last group of cottages was sold and we expanded the community. The dynamics changed, . . . and some women came in who weren't compatible with our values, such as the importance of consensus decision-making." Some women felt that the original residents tended to be autocratic and resistant to change.

Emily added, "We got together weekly to deal with our conflicts and issues. . . . It transformed my life, made me dig deep inside about how I really wanted to live. We formed a bond that we still have to this day. It will always be there because we struggled through issues, we struggled through conflicts . . . to come up with the fairest, kindest way to deal with the issues. To me this is a big part of feminism. . . . Now they don't have that. They don't meet to resolve issues."

Fayann continues, "For someone like that to stay and evolve and be there, it takes somebody with a commitment to do that work, a commitment to the idea, and willing to do what it takes to make that happen."

Barbara said, "We had a process that worked for us for ten years. It was called 'group' and it met every Thursday night. You didn't have to come. We had as a bottom line that if you had a conflict that you couldn't resolve with another woman in the community, we asked you to bring it to group." She explained that when they expanded, some of the newer women wanted this process changed, and they were unable to find an equitable solution. Some of the women who lived at Pagoda felt that there were problems around class issues which were not raised, never mind dealt with. The fact of some women having more and some having less, whether materially, time-wise, or emotionally, was a bone of contention.[4]

As the land around them became developed, the result was a lack of space for them to expand to accommodate new projects such as a residential living space for long-lived women, a project called Crone's Nest, discussed since the 1980s, but that has never manifested. There were also problems with business and

---

4   The class issues came up in an email to Rose Norman from Rainbow Williams (September 23, 2014) and Vicki Wengrow (September 27, 2014), as part of the process of reviewing this essay.

bookkeeping, and with environmental issues brought about by climate change.

Over the next decade, women came and women went. The land developed, the climate and the community changed, "progress" happened, and many of the original members felt that Pagoda was no longer for them. Six members sold their cottages and moved to the mountains of North Alabama where they started another kind of women's community in northeast Alabama, Alapine Village [see p. 146].

In the mid-1980s, Canadian artist Myriam Fougère came to Pagoda to do a show of her sculptures in exchange for a free week there. She stayed for two months. For $10 a month, she became a member. She moved from Quebec to Brooklyn and traveled around the United States showing her work, but she returned to Pagoda several times a year. In 1987, she bought a cottage with Lin Daniels, and whatever her schedule, she continues to come to Pagoda for two weeks every year. As to the collective process, she says, "There were always controversies, but I stayed away from them. . . . My activism was mostly art. At The Pagoda there were lots of arguments/discussions, and meetings that would last hours and hours. I've been to some of those meetings, but I was never a resident and was never in the thick of it. You know, I could give my opinion, and if I didn't want to stay for the five-hour meeting, I could always go away because I was not a real part of it. That was how I liked it to be, because, . . . like Irene Weiss says in my film [*Lesbiana*], we don't know how to create community. I feel like I don't either, and it *is* really hard, and it *is* painful, and complicated. I stayed away from the complication to be able to enjoy it. . . . I didn't want to choose sides and be against this one or that one."

In 1984, Rainbow Williams celebrated her fiftieth birthday by moving to Pagoda. In 1988, she and seven other Lesbians raised the money for the last four cottages and ocean lots. Those last four cottages came to be known as "North Pagoda," and the cottages and three empty lots were bought by Paulette Armistead,

Nancy Breeze, Ann Harmon, Marilyn Murphy, Irene Weiss, Earthstar, Rainbow, and Marie. These were the people who did not want to attend long weekly meetings. Rainbow believes this is partly a class issue: "If you can afford to spend five hours in a meeting, you must be independently supported."[5]

Pagoda women living at Alapine, taken after a group interview about Pagoda, April 13, 2013. Back row (l to r): Barbara Lieu, Jean Adele, Fayann Schmidt, Ellen Spangler, Morgana MacVicar. Seated on floor: Rose Norman (interviewer), Emily Greene.

The Pagoda Temple of Love bought the swimming pool by selling "lifetime" pool memberships. Rainbow recalls, "That 'lifetime' would last eleven years due to a decision in 1999 to sell the Center and the pool." The original Pagoda women, who had moved to Alapine, had new mortgages to pay. "A meeting was held," Rainbow continues, "and offers presented. Only one offered the option of Lesbian buyers to the building that housed the departing Temple of Love," which, along with its tax-free status as a church, also was moved to Alapine. The Temple was purchased

---

5 Email to Rose Norman from Rainbow Williams, September 23, 2014.

by Fairy Godmothers, Inc.—Rena, Rainbow, Liz, and Marie. They "ran the building as a resort rental for four years unsuccessfully, then as two apartments, up and down, unsuccessfully, then in 2008 it was offered as a single house rental top to bottom, and we found happy hippie tenants with a year's lease. Taxes and maintenance kept us broke, and tensions were high." It is currently for sale.

"And the twelve little cottages?" Rainbow concludes, "Still there, and they get cuter every day, with individual decks, porches, flowers, and bright paint. All belong to dykes except for a couple of gay-friendly folks who appreciate being there. As each is individually owned, the cottage owner may sell or rent as she needs to, and there is no community control over them. They are rarely available as short term rentals, and even more rarely on the market to sell. It's quite a stable neighborhood, with plenty of old hippie values, and familiar faces of twenty years' residence."

SO YOU THINK YOU WANT TO LIVE IN COMMUNITY

Barbara Lieu

Sung to the tune of "I Am the Very Model
of a Modern Major General" by Gilbert & Sullivan

We are the very model of a Lesbian community.
Our diff'rences they pale when we compare them to our unity.
We strive to keep our meetings short because we value brevity;
But often they go long in spite of what we want to be

And when we disagree it seems to be with some intensity.
We try our best, but must confess, we lose congeniality.
We practice NVC[1] to help increase communication skills.
We think if we get better it will surely help to solve our ills.
When resolution happens, all around the circle feel the thrill.
And once again we each commit to try our very best until
Our diff'rences they pale when we compare them to our unity.
We are the very model of a Lesbian community.

All: We are the very model of a what community?
We are the very model of a what community?
We are the very model of a can-we-get-it-right community

We all have left our past behind and moved to this vicinity.
We hoped to find ones of like mind and of compatibility.
Our diff'rences they pale when we compare them to our unity.
We are the very model of a Lesbian community.

All: Our diff'rences they pale when we compare them to our unity.
We are the very model of a Lesbian community

---

1   Non-Violent Communication.

SUGARLOAF WOMEN'S VILLAGE: "SOME GROUND TO STAND ON"

Rose Norman

"Living simply is not always easy, and living collectively is definitely not easy. There's nothing in our experience to teach us how to do that. And we're still trying to define what we are as a community. But because Barbara and Jane left these properties, we have some ground to stand on."

—Blue Lunden[1]

In 1976, Barbara Deming, peace and social justice activist and writer, bought the land that was to become Sugarloaf Women's Village, a small women's community on Sugarloaf Key, northeast of Key West, Florida. She had moved from New York to Sugarloaf Key for health reasons after being seriously injured in a car wreck in 1971. She came with her life partner, the artist, poet, and activist Jane Verlaine, and their friends, the writers Andrea Dworkin and John Stoltenberg.[2] There were two houses and a guest cottage on that first 100 × 150 feet lot she bought near the end of a suburban drive, bordered by a canal that leads to the turquoise ocean. Deming and Verlaine lived in one house, Dworkin and Stoltenberg in the two-story house next door, and a parade of visitors came to stay at the guest cottage, mostly their friends from New York, writers, artists, and activists.

Blue Lunden was a radical Lesbian activist from New Orleans, who had moved to Sugarloaf from New York City after visiting

---

1 Closing words of Joyce Warshow's documentary film *Some Ground to Stand On: The Story of Blue Lunden*, 1998, available from Women Make Movies (order no. W99599).

2 Dworkin and Stoltenberg left a year later (Bonnie Netherton interview). She identified as Lesbian and he as gay, but they were together 31 years and married in 1998 (*Wikipedia*).

Barbara Deming and Jane Verlaine in 1981, with her life partner Sky Vanderlinde. When she was dying of cancer in 1999, Blue Lunden set up Sugarloaf Women's Land Trust, Inc., to govern and protect Sugarloaf Women's Village. Blue had inherited the property when Jane Verlaine died in 1992, and Jane had inherited it when Barbara Deming died in 1984. By 1999, the one lot had expanded to six 100 × 150 feet lots and included two additional houses on the lots facing the street behind the original houses, two guest cottages, a campground, and three wooded lots. Within this space, residents and visitors created a feeling of playful sanctuary, with profuse tropical flowers, orange trees, an outdoor shower under an old banyan tree, and familiar house plants growing outside year-round in the lush shade. The undeveloped lots provide primitive camping in the poisonwood forest.

Photo courtesy of Bonnie Netherton

Bonnie Netherton with Barbara Deming during the 1983 peace walk from Gainesville to Key West.

When they formed the land trust in 1999, Sugarloaf was already well known in Lesbian circles as a wonderful place to visit, a place that had sponsored consciousness-raising groups, dream groups, weekly women's potlucks, and all manner of activism, especially the peace activism and social justice writings that were Barbara Deming's life work, the domestic violence activism that was Jane Verlaine's passion, and the LGBT activism that Blue Lunden added to the mix.

The statement of purpose that still guides the trustees reads:

> Barbara Deming's life and work is the spirit and guide to the purposes of Sugarloaf Women's Village. Her dedication and conviction that nonviolence as a way of life can and will promote world peace and equality inspires our lives. Her belief that one must resist injustice and abuse of power, racial and sexual inequalities and the hegemony of the nuclear and military industrial complex with love and non-violent struggle guides our work. As a community we want to continue in her tradition of doing and supporting political work, the empowerment of women and activism and to encourage the activist in us all. We share her dream that wimmin will combine the concept of non-violence with feminist practice. We strive to build the "beloved community" and bring her light to the future.
> We dedicate our endeavors to our foresisters Barbara Deming, Jane Verlaine, Ruth Dreamdigger, and Blue Lunden. May we walk their walk.[3]

Much has changed since Blue died in 1999. The community activism and frequent social events—dream group, CR groups—that were so much a part of life there in the 1980s and 1990s are no longer, as the organizers and participants have died or moved away. But the property is very well maintained, and much energy now goes into improving and upgrading visitor accommodations

---

3 Quoted from an unpublished document at Sugarloaf Women's Village, part of the legal documentation of the land trust.

and expanding the circle of friends who are visiting members of the community. Current residents are dedicated to making the land available to as many women as possible.

Here we have compiled some of the stories of residents and others from interviews with Bonnie Netherton and Connie Tarpley recorded at Sugarloaf in 2013[4] and from memories contributed by frequent visitors.

Bonnie Netherton on the Land Trust and Living on the Land

Bonnie Netherton has been a permanent resident of Sugarloaf Women's Village since 2006, and she visited Sugarloaf off and on from 1983 on. She participated in creating the Sugarloaf Women's Land Trust that took over the property after Blue's death, serving as one of the first trustees.

In 1983, I was moving to Key West from St. Simon's Island. I had stored all my furniture and packed my car full of belongings with my Windsurfer on the roof. I stopped at Pagoda [in St. Augustine] on the way, and spent a few days there. Barbara Lieu and Lavender Lieu told me I had to meet Barbara Deming. So they called Barbara and gave me an introduction to her and let her know that I would be coming. When I got here, Barbara came right up to my car, looked in the window, and said "I believe the Goddess has sent you to us." I wasn't even out of my car yet! (Interview 2013)

Connie Tarpley

Connie Tarpley, who lives in Key West, was one of the original board members of the Sugarloaf Women's Land Trust. Although she did not live at Sugarloaf, she visited often, and was a lifelong friend of the artist Vogel (d. 2009), and in a relationship with Vogel from 1982 to 1995. Vogel lived at Sugarloaf from about 1984 to 1999.

---

4   Rose Norman interviewed Connie Tarpley at the community house in Sugarloaf Women's Village on November 7, 2013. In addition to over nine hours of recorded interviews that Rose Norman conducted with Bonnie Netherton at Sugarloaf Women's Village, November 4–7, 2013, this essay draws on Bonnie's postings about Sugarloaf to the Landdykes online discussion group in 2012.

I met Jane [Verlaine] probably first, because she was involved with a group of women seeking to start a shelter for battered women. Our first work together involved creating temporary safe houses for battered women. She invited me to a CR group at Sugarloaf in the very late 1970s around 1978 or 1979.

RN: *I'm wondering at what point Barbara and Jane began to think about this as women's land.*

CT: For me, that was Blue! She came from New York where she had an apartment that was open to any woman who needed to be there. I think the need to have an open apartment and open land sprang from her feeling she didn't have a place, having been orphaned and raised [in New Orleans] by an aunt. She very much wanted to have women's land, and a place where women could feel safe, and I think she was the real driving force. Before Blue came, it was very intellectual, and I loved that—the people who came through here were peace activists from Chile and Argentina, and writers, people who this girl from Tennessee had never been exposed to. Blue brought a different flavor to it. It was more about community with her. Not that Barbara and Jane weren't about community, but I felt like Blue was the one who brought the sense of community.

Bonnie Netherton on Blue Lunden

When Barbara met Blue, they just loved each other. They were both activists, both in the peace and freedom movement. When Blue Lunden and Sky VanDerlinde first visited in 1981, they came for dinner and stayed for three weeks. Blue and Sky had a little Teardrop trailer that they towed behind their car, and they stayed in that. Then Barbara wanted Blue to live here, and the house next to what is now the community house came on the market, and Barbara bought it for Blue and Sky. She put three names on the deed for the new house: Barbara, Jane, and Blue. Blue and Sky paid rent on it while Barbara was alive, from about 1982. The following year, Barbara bought the house next door (which shared the same

100 × 150 feet lot as Blue and Sky's house) to allow for community expansion. Blue's vision was that it would be a community house and space for visitors, but Barbara wanted it to be rented to new residents, as evidenced by her efforts to rent the house to Quinn Dilkes and then to me. In the end, both purposes came about, with Ruth Dreamdigger becoming a permanent resident and making her space available to visitors as well.

Blue always had visitors in her house, too. She had three bedrooms, so there was always someone there, and she opened her kitchen to whoever wanted to use it. That was Blue.

Photo courtesy of Connie Tarpley

Sugarloaf residents (l to r) Blue Lunden,
Ruth Dreamdigger, and Vogel (before 1999).

Connie Tarpley on Barbara Deming, Blue Lunden, and Community

I knew of Barbara from reading about her in *Ms. Magazine* even before I met her at Sugarloaf. I loved Barbara Deming. I learned a lot from her, most importantly deep listening. She turned her attention to all women, no matter their social standing or intellectual ability or even sexual preference. Of course, she started out as a peace activist and a champion of civil rights. There is no doubt that she was a Lesbian-feminist activist. I believe that the community was her dream, but I personally believe that her focus was on the larger community, the world. I began to hear the dream of the Sugarloaf Community talked about more after Blue arrived. To me the community appeared to come alive after Blue, Claudia, and Xylena arrived. There's a certain spirit to it [community], and one is intellectual. The other is a spirit that does not exclude the intellectual but embraces all expressions of strong women, a spirit that brought everyone together, that got things going. Out of this sprang some strife, but I think that was a necessary part of growth. There was a period of time, it seemed to me, when the community was just women living in separate houses, and that doesn't mean there wasn't some community going on, just a different type of community.

Barbara Deming was wonderful, a deep, deep listener. In that way, she was very much a community person. I think that's something that Blue shared with her. When she turned her attention to you, you really felt heard and valued.

Bonnie Netherton and Corky Culver on Blue Lunden, Ruth Dreamdigger, and the Unitarian Universalist Church

Bonnie: Blue and Ruth were both active in the Unitarian Universalist church here, and at that time it didn't have a minister, so congregation members led whatever services they had. That congregation was a platform for Blue, one that she enjoyed. I think she started doing that after Ruth moved here.

Corky: I went to one of those UU sessions that Blue did on women's spirituality. It was incredible. She talked about how much it meant to her to hear the name of a goddess, having come from a tradition of only male gods. It was empowering and beautiful. It valued women in an important way, instead of making them subservient or dangerous. Then she passed out to the congregation slips of paper with names of goddesses and a description of them, and asked each person to stand up and read from it in the voice of the goddess, e.g., "I am Diana, goddess of the forest. I treasure wildlife and deer." It brought tears to my eyes because it was in a church, and I had that same background of feeling left out, of feeling that things I valued like nature and women had been kept out of the church I went to, and there had been judgment and no joy. And here was a service in a church where I was hearing such beautiful things. Then Ruth Dreamdigger got up and read from Ntozake Shange's poem:

> "i found god in myself
> and i loved her
> i loved her fiercely"

Star Woodward remembers Barbara Deming's death[5]

Bonnie Netherton took me to Sugarloaf shortly after we had both moved to Key West in about 1983. I would go up for the community meeting/potlucks on Wednesday nights. About a year after I moved to the Keys, I moved to Sugarloaf. Blue helped me make a bedroom out of the back porch of the community house. I changed my name to Star while I was living there. Sugarloaf is a formative part of my Lesbian life.

Around the time I moved in, Barbara went to New York City for cancer treatments. After a few months, Barbara moved back home, to die. There were women from all over the place coming to see her, to say good-bye. I remember famous Lesbians like Minnie Bruce Pratt and Adrienne Rich coming, but there were lots more over those three weeks before Barbara died. In the last week, about twenty women were there, and we would all go over to Barbara's house and crowd into her tiny living room and sing to her. At her request! Spirituals and peace songs, sometimes in rounds. She also asked a lot of us to come

---

5   Email from Star to Rose Norman, 8-27-14.

over one at a time, to give us a little something. Mine was a tiny wooden box from Amsterdam.

Cybilla Hawk on a Croning at Sugarloaf[6]

Cybilla Hawk lived in South Central Florida for many years, and began visiting Sugarloaf in the 1980s, after Barbara Deming's death.

There was a croning at Sugarloaf that I attended [in the early 1990s, before 1992] when we croned Blue Lunden, Jane Verlaine, and Ruth Dreamdigger. That whole weekend we spent either at one of their houses or one of the beaches where you can camp. They told their life stories. Oh, my god! I wish I had a recording of that. Each one told these amazing things they'd done in their lives. Then we had this big feast and decorated Blue's house with stars that we hung from the ceiling. Afterward, we had a ritual around a fire outdoors back of Blue's house. A night heron came and landed on the back end of Blue's house and stayed for the whole ceremony. We decided that was Barbara [Deming] coming to the ritual. I almost get shivers remembering that, as it was so magical.

Bonnie Netherton on Sally Willowbee

Sally Willowbee has been a really important person here. One thing she contributed was putting the bug in Blue's ear about forming a land trust. Sally was a good fundraiser, and she raised the money to buy the land across the street. She refused to put that lot in Blue's name. She formed the land trust with that land, and when Blue died, all of her property went into that land trust. Blue was conflicted about having a land trust, but I think that in her heart she wanted it that way. She was just afraid it wouldn't be taken care of. One time she said to me, "I'm afraid if I make it a land trust, they'll kick me out!"

---

6 From an interview that Rose Norman did with Cybilla Hawk on August 23, 2014, in Huntsville, Alabama.

An Ending, and a Beginning

Even though it did not begin as a Landyke community, in many ways, Sugarloaf Women's Village was the beneficiary of the Landyke movement because so many Landykes had visited there and were able to bring their knowledge and experience to help Blue Lunden set up the land trust that has kept the community alive to this day, welcoming Lesbians year-round, and creating a way for Lesbians to afford to live in community. According to the Sugarloaf website, "The land and houses are held in trust for all Lesbians, and all women are welcome to visit. Any Lesbian can apply for residency" (sugarloafwomensvillage.com/Herstory.html).

Today the land has four permanent residents. Rita Otis and Bridget Lynch are a couple who live in the two-story house, the house that Andrea Dworkin first lived in. In summer 2014, Bonnie Netherton moved from the house where Barbara Deming and Jane Verlaine (and later Sandy Hagan) lived, to the house where Blue Lunden lived, next to the community house. A brand-new resident, Corrie Garnet, now lives in what is still known as "Barbara and Jane's house."

All four of the permanent residents serve on the board of the land trust, plus four other trustees. Bonnie Netherton keeps up with the Sugarloaf Women's Village email and website (www.sugarloafwomensvillage.com), makes visitor reservations, and welcomes visitors to the property. The number of annual visitors has increased from 60 in 2010, to 80 in 2011, 105 in 2012, 135 in 2013, and 145 in 2014.

Bonnie Netherton on Sugarloaf's Uniqueness

Sugarloaf is unique in that we exist in the Florida Keys, which is a magnet for visitors. Because of this, it has become very expensive to live or visit here. We provide a place where women can live and visit very reasonably and comfortably. Most visitors are grateful for the opportunity to spend some time here, and current residents are very grateful to have a home here. A resident can live out her life here if she chooses, and there have actually been five women who did just that, with four of them dying at home here in their own beds, cared for by loving women until the end of their days.[7] Their spirits embrace and enliven Sugarloaf Women's Village and are a beacon for those of us here today. I think they help us to stay in appreciation mode.

7 Barbara Deming, Blue Lunden, Ruth Dreamdigger, and Sandy Hagan died on the land. Jane Verlaine died in hospital, but her ashes are in the urn in the peace garden, with those of Barbara, Blue, Ruth, and others.

SPIRAL: SPIRITED, POWERFUL, INDEPENDENT, RADICAL AMAZON LESBIANS

Kate Ellison

When I visited SPIRAL in rural south-central Kentucky with my partner Jes for the first time in 1983, Mary and Lucina were living in a farmhouse next to the land. It was a chilly October day, with a mist that never seemed to lift. While Mary and Lucina were at work, we walked the old road into SPIRAL soaking in the silence, the rocky rough terrain, the sweet mountain spring. There was a log cabin, with a massive rock fireplace and hand-hewn chestnut logs steeped in history. Across the road was a pole barn, smelling faintly of the tobacco leaves that had been hung there every year. If you walked long enough, up the steep logging road hugging the ridge, you came to Pine Knobs, a rock outcropping with a vista of forest for miles around, nothing else.

Jes and I were traveling cross-country, recovering from our first attempt to create wimmin's land, and the death of Jes' father. In 1978, I bought twenty acres in Rappahannock County, northern Virginia, with two other women in order to start a New-Age organization for protecting children. Only an hour out of DC, this was secluded woodland, with access to a paved road, and a creek along one border. When the others dropped out, I continued to make payments, and in the spring of 1981, my friend Lynn asked if she and Phenix could camp out on that land. I said, "sure—it must be time to start a new land collective." They set up tents and a campfire, and a group of five women came together to form "Turtleland," because Phenix, part Native American, told of a tradition that when two women make love, a turtle is born.

Some of us were members of a Dianic coven called Circle of Isis, and held ceremonies there whenever possible. A group of ten to fifteen women could be free to drum and dance naked, chanting the names of the goddess, outside in the night without fear. Returning to the ancient goddess, returning to the earth, we felt alive and whole.

Like so many feminists at the time, we struggled with race and class consciousness, and these misunderstandings broke up the collective. Jes and I left the collective in the fall of 1983, handing over the land and $2000 of Jes' new inheritance. We climbed in our truck and took off to visit friends and faraway Lesbian lands. Eventually, the group disbanded, and responsibility for the land payments came back to me.

SPIRAL was the last stop of our 1983 trip. It was a pristine land, about 250 acres with three fields totaling about five acres, but mostly woods. The farmers who previously owned it had grown tobacco and soybeans, and logged the woods. They cut trees about every ten years, treating the woods as a crop, so there had been no clear cutting, and the trees with real character (twisted, or with lower branches, or hollow) were left to live out their lives.

The original SPIRAL collective formed in 1980 and grew to about twenty-five women at the time they bought this piece, for $50,000 in 1981. Lucina (a nurse) went with the only other woman who had a respectable job, to get the bank loan. The down payment came from fund-raising, like selling "Momma Corn" at the Michigan Womyn's Festival.

Bringing the dream into the physical caused huge stresses, and most of the wimmin drifted away. Some had difficulty with the concept of "ownership" of the land, when Mother Earth is whole unto herself. A core group of three to five was trying to hang onto the possibility of ownership, as payments ballooned with fourteen percent interest. When Jes and I decided to become a part of SPIRAL in 1985, we used the money from the sale of Turtleland to help bring down the principal.

Jes and I spent our vacation time each spring at SPIRAL. Mary's house was being built, then Joy's, and there were occasional meetings of about ten women. Jes and I finally moved to Kentucky in 1988, with a sense that leaving the city was leaving patriarchy behind, embarking on a completely new female existence. It was very physically demanding to live there, even with electricity and occasionally running water. We heated with wood, and there were no flush toilets. The land, so rugged, was not very accessible at all.

Buying land, creating a structure both legal and collective, consumed the first several years of SPIRAL's existence. Building houses, sheds, and roads took many more years. Finding ways to have an income even longer. Over time, about thirty wimmin's lives touched at SPIRAL, with about ten who stayed for periods of years. Eventually, on October 25, 1991, the mortgage was fully paid, and SPIRAL belonged to our land trust.

Mary Hoelterhoff driving the 1949 Ford tractor Kate brought to SPIRAL. Mary used the tractor to grade the road and create gardens. She had the front bucket added. Mary, Kate, and a few others used it to bushhog the fields.

By 1994, various wimmin had built (but not all finished) seven houses, both large and small. Two wimmin built at the road's steep end, installing solar panels for electricity. Lia learned wiring and battery installation, and Gina brought her horse, some goats, and chickens. We all worked on the Star Hut, using a kit to create a five-sided geodesic dome. Bo worked mostly by herself to create a six-sided, two-story home, with water catchment high enough that it could run to the sink for washing. Susan built her home organically with rocks she collected, and cement she mixed. Joy's house was as much outside deck as inside space. All had big, south-facing windows and no need for curtains.

Together, we built houses and roads, sharing and learning skills that usually only men could acquire. We did all the cement work, carpentry, wiring, plumbing, and roofing. Chain saws, circular saws, ladders, a tractor—these were our own tools, and we relished their use. We drew plans, mixed concrete, framed walls; we raised several houses from ground to roof. My house was two stories, with four bedrooms, for me, Jes, Loret, and a guest. It was slow, but I enjoyed it more than any job I've had. Building brought a great sense of pride and accomplishment, and challenged stereotypes of women's work.

Working together on my house meant I was in charge that day. Working together on Mary's house meant she was in charge. We shared, listened, yelled, cried, and sometimes walked away. But the houses we built are still standing.

Mary's house is really tall, with a garage below two stories of living space. It is anchored and warmed on the south side by a greenhouse, and has a cistern, a well, and a cedar hot tub heated with wood. Her house overlooks the largest field, and there she began farming, eventually creating a CSA, where she had LNR-funded apprentices.[1] She was a mechanic, an organic farmer, and a builder.

Travelers came to visit, mostly young dykes, bringing news and new ideas from other communities. It was intellectually stimulating

1 Community Supported Agriculture: CSA subscribers pay at the onset of the growing season for a share of the anticipated harvest; once harvesting begins, they receive weekly shares of vegetables, fruit, herbs, flowers, etc. LNR is Lesbian Natural Resources (see story p. 173).

in our relative isolation, and they were generally eager to help with the building and farming projects. They often self-identified as separatist, which SPIRAL residents did not. We walked a fine line, finding what we could in common with local farmers, while taking pride in all we did without relying on men. For me, separatists honed a hard edge, pure in ideology, yet hostile to other points of view. Every visitor was welcomed with a potluck and long discussions that might be contentious, and were always interesting.

Photo courtesy of Kate Ellison

Kate Ellison working with circular saw
on one of the houses at SPIRAL.

Living in the country, far from any city, as a group of self-sufficient women, was a radical act. It was anathema to call in a man for a job we could eventually figure out how to do ourselves. We could be in charge of our lives and take control of a situation if we needed to. It was thrilling. The local people were hard-pressed to take in what we meant. Our neighbors, farmers who had rarely left the county, were amazed. "The personal is political," feminism said, and for us that meant living without the smothering protection of men, valuing each other, and seeing the sacred feminine in every tree and stream.

We tried to ensure that every womyn's voice was heard, and that we could all support the decisions we made. With almost no experience, meetings were very long, arduous events. Feminist process was crucial to recovering our voices, the new idea that each womyn was important. Consensus decision-making worked for a number of years, although sometimes we had to call in mediators.

We wanted the community to grow, and sought new members, while knowing it was a huge decision to leave city and job for essentially the unknown. One of the small cabins we built was designated "the REM" for Resident Exploring Membership, and also rapid eye movement, the dream state. A newcomer could stay on the land through the four seasons, experience the life, and dream about how and where she would build. We needed her to spend some time with us, getting to know each womyn, before embarking on what we hoped would be a lifetime commitment. Probably a dozen women entered this process, leaving before the year was up.

Eventually, I came to realize that you couldn't really walk out on patriarchy. It's inside us. The ways that we had been belittled, or not appreciated as whole human beings, the ways that we were mistreated growing up; we brought all that with us to the land. So we had the same kind of power struggles, ego trips, and misunderstandings that everyone else has. We weren't that great at rising above our backgrounds, but we never abandoned the process of listening to each other and speaking our truths.

No one at SPIRAL had much money, and with few exceptions, we were unsuccessful finding work in town. We joined the food co-op (buying club) with the local back-to-the-land hippies, meeting the Frontier Coop truck at the town's armory once a month. Jes and I spent our savings on building materials, and Jes was able to work as a home-health nurse (LPN) while I was building our house (with numerous visitors and community members). Mary spent most growing seasons working in her father's nursery in suburban Chicago, went to college, and began her CSA. Joy held a number of social work jobs, went back to school, and eventually returned to the city. Jes and I developed a business based on her skill as an herbal healer, and the herbal tinctures we made. Torii taught Reiki. Bo, Susan, and most of the other REMs survived on very little money, often from arts and crafts. Bo and I learned rag-rug weaving on borrowed looms. For about a year, some of us were part of a craft store in the closest town, selling our own and other people's "crafts." Gina and I began cleaning houses and mowing lawns around 1998, and REMs Amber and Annie joined us for a while.

The Holy Grail for this self-sufficient remote community was always a cottage industry that could make living here financially feasible. A hammock business brought us this opportunity. Twin Oaks Community in Virginia had the national contract with Pier One to make thousands of hammocks, and had developed efficient tools and methods they wanted to share with other intentional communities. Their residents, tired of making so many hammocks, were eager to supply, train, and pay us to do this work. Joy had moved away years earlier, and with her permission, "the Joy House" became hammock central. We each learned all the skills, but it was faster to make many of the same part at once. Some were drawn to weaving, some harness making, some putting it all together, etc.

Shared work, shared income—it was a dream come true that became a nightmare. How to pay for the trip to Twin Oaks to pick up supplies and deliver hammocks? Who could use what supplies on what schedule? We were paid $17 and change per hammock, and we kept track of our hours, estimating two hours per hammock. The agreement on how to pay ourselves took months of meetings.

We each came from different backgrounds and had differing relationships with money and views toward sharing any resource. Sharing our financial fate created the very worst fights. We came from nuclear families, but we tried to live and work in an egalitarian, tribal, non-patriarchal way. We were fierce in our idealism and struggled to make our dreams a reality.

Holly Near talked about wimmin who were "cultural workers," and she mainly meant the work of creating feminist art and music. I think Landykes are cultural workers, creators of a new way of life, living feminism in daily life. I have said we failed, because we could not sustain the struggle. The project grew creatively for more than two decades. Our listing in *Shewolf's Directory* now says "For Sale."

DREAMING

Kate Ellison

On the occasion of falling in love, leaving the city,
and moving to womyn's land, 2-19-88.

I reached out
from my safe, lonely shelter
to touch
    NEWNESS:
    Wondering, opening,
    I came to embrace you.

    Our wombspace became fertile
    with the ova of our dreams

Elephant-like,
the gestation of hope
lumbered out of time
toward birth

We prepared a spiral nest
of sturdy womyn-loving truths,
elegant ecological twigs,
softly lined with fine
feminist feathers.

Pulling for perfection,
we squirm to avoid
patriarchal prickles poking through . . .

Desire and fear
highlight each tentative movement
in stark shadow and bright focus.

Choice lies in the past:
Both of us have birthed
dreams stillborn
or recognized error and aborted.

Now this dream comes to term.

Midwives to each other,
we are dream-coach, healer, crone
    TREMORS—breathe deep
    CONTRACTIONS—bear down
    CONTRADICTIONS—keep flowing

The birth canal opens.
Dreamchild, EMERGE
your moment is NOW.

FULL HARVEST

Kate Ellison

(*Written 1991*)

Abundance by design:
The Mother's, not mine.
She fills my basket with her mystery.

I planned to harvest beans and grain,
Knowledge, strength, a job!
We needed rain.

Aching for water,
I watched crops wither, trees wilt,
Grasses rustle in dry streambeds.
Unemployment lingered.

Along the hot dusty road
I failed to notice
That flowers prevail—
In gold and purple splendor
Hardy "weeds" prepare wild seeds in profusion,
Their beauty stored for next season,
Their cycle fulfilled.

Along the hot dusty road
My itchy country dog pants and plays.
She gives me dog lips, abundant loyalty,
And deep in her dark eyes—humor.
She understands—do I?

I could miss the Mother's bounty,
Her subtle opportunity to respond.
She's not unknowable,
Just not quite the known.

Grandma snake shakes her rattle,
Keeps me on my toes!
I stop, I wait
It's her flow I need to know.
She slithers away in silence
She asks not for surrender,
Just for presence, in her NOW.

Tiny turtle on the run
Busy with the journey of a lifetime,
Undaunted by cat or womyn,
Filled with purpose—
Has the Mother given me less?

Heat of day gives way to nightly cooling fog.
I curl into our nest,
A soft enfolding contentment.

I fill my basket with unplanned abundance,
The Mother's harvest:
        Wild seeds
        Country canine humor
            Rattlesnake dance
                Turtle logic
                Womyn touch

It is enough.

WHAT IT CAME DOWN TO

Kate Ellison

(*On leaving SPIRAL, 2003*)

You yelled at me because you feel invisible,
scream of agreements that I broke.
You accuse me of violating you,
    stepping on your needs.
You force me to stop at your wall of pain—
Speak to me from your heart and I will listen.

If you feel invisible, show yourself.
If you have a boundary, draw it in the sand.
I can't hear the arguments
you have with me inside your own head.
I can't see you standing tall inside your own house.

Write me a letter
Make me a sign
Draw me a picture
Speak from your heart and I will listen.

I feel your anger rising,
your venom sprays and burns.
Are you asking for help?
Should I schedule a meeting now?

I wish I was immune
I wish I had a hard shell
when you hurt me, I wish I could feel
something beyond my own pain.

Speak your heart and I will listen.
Don't evaluate my failures
Don't inflate your anger with rationalizations.
Tell me you are afraid or lost
Tell me you feel out of control—
I will listen, I will hear you.

Tell me you care
Tell me you need to talk
I will listen, I will answer.

I want to speak my heart too
I need you to hear my pain—will you listen?
When we both feel heard,
    It will be a brand new day.

SILVER CIRCLE SANCTUARY: BEGINNINGS AND LEGACY

B. Leaf Cronewrite

"Our dream is to create a community of interdependent wimmin on and off the land working on changing our patriarchal programming regarding inferiority feelings, competition, compulsivity, tragic life tapes, deprivation mindset, possessiveness, body shame, manipulative behaviors, intolerance, and spiritual beliefs."
Silver Circle, *Maize* 4 (1985): 10

Rose Norman interviewed Gwen Demeter and Gail Atkins at Womonwrites, October 13, 2013. B. Leaf Cronewrite interviewed them at Silver Circle on November 18, 2013. B. Leaf has combined information from both interviews. Gwen is speaking unless otherwise noted.

Beginnings

In 1975, before Silver Circle, we [Gail Atkins and Gwen Demeter] met at a NOW meeting in Memphis. Our romance continued on and off until we got together permanently in 1980.

Our dream of sharing women's land began in 1980. While living communally in Memphis, we formed a spirituality circle to call the land to us. Maybe twenty women were part of the circle, including Georganne/WolfSpider, Alicia, Em, and Sue. Some were interested in land, and some were just there for ritual.

At a ritual in 1982, we put out what we were looking for. Gail said she wanted it within a week, adding, "I'm not looking. They're going to have to call me." And they did! The realtor determined that a gas line that they had feared was on the property was a mile away, so the call was made.

We drove south to Marshall County, Mississippi, to look at the land on Valentine weekend in February 1982. We walked through a cane break that tractors had made since the land was being leased to grow beans. Gail said "this is it" before she walked down to a clearing where the house is now. We bought the land the next week, paying $15,000 cash. Pat's business fronted an interest-free loan for $5000, Alicia had $5000, and I paid $5000 cash. It was forty acres with nothing on it but pine trees, hills, cactus, sand, dry creek, a wet creek part of the year. Electricity poles ran through the property. From February until Thanksgiving, we hauled water using milk jugs from Keel's Country Store three miles away.

The early days were rocky with no vehicle access until a culvert was put in. We parked our truck on the road and pitched tents on the land, but the former owner, Odell, threatened to have the truck towed. When Odell offered to bushhog an access path through the tall grass on our property, we thought he was being neighborly. We were hopeful that a better relationship with him would result. Instead he cleared out a privacy barrier between our tents and the road. His actions were a disappointment that continued our mistrust of him.

Through the years, we have had just a few instances of vandalism. Tools, the dinner bell, and a sign were stolen over the years. Georganne patrolled our road with a shotgun for a while. In 1994, two carloads of fraternity boys stole a sign and the mailbox. When they came down the driveway, Gail shot in the air. We heard later at a local restaurant that "the big one will shoot you," which gave us a laugh.

Naming the Land

We thought of naming the land Pleiades to represent the seven women who were part of the original land group: Georganne/WolfSpider, Alicia, Robin, Pat, Annabel, and us. Instead, practicality produced the name. We put up a mailbox and had some silver paint, and Gail painted a silver circle on it so a delivery truck could find us. Seven women's names were on the deed with the legal right of survivorship, so none of our relatives could inherit from us.

In later years, the original five chose not to live on the land, and we two became the sole owners.

Living on the Land

We moved into a tent on the land with our queen-sized bed. Because it was the rainiest year in a long time, we bought a wood camper shell to put on Gail's red Ford F150 truck. We moved the bed into the back of the truck, with a manual typewriter, and a drip coffeepot on a shelf behind the cab, and the two cats and one dog, and a radio on the side.

When electric lines were downed by a storm, and disconnected from the transformer, we knew the electric would be out for about a week. We took advantage and pulled power without codes or permits. Having electricity and a hastily built dome kitchen helped us survive the first year.

Pat and Annabel did not plan to live there. It was Pat's survivor place in case things went wrong in Memphis, an earthquake or something. They did not build anything immediately, but helped us with supplies like boots and down jackets, other supplies, and Pat sent food. We didn't think we needed their supplies, but they came in handy!

Robin and Alicia spent a cold night in a tent and decided not to live on the land, instead moving to California. Early on, Georganne lived in a tent, eventually staying until 1986 when she moved to San Francisco. Her partner Bluejay lived in a van for a couple of months and helped out. So there were four of us on the land the first year.

Buildings

At first, Georganne built a very small, 8 × 2 feet tool shed since there were no other structures yet. The kitchen was a clothesline with plastic over it, tent-wise. We put in a small garden in the spring, trying to grow asparagus and snow peas, and everything else. We also tried to have a garden in the back field where there was more sun, but there was no water back there.

In June, Gail and Georganne built a dome kitchen. Sue donated some nice hardwood for the floor. There wasn't enough lumber for a roof overhang to keep rain from splashing the house. Years later, Ayla Heartsong repaired the outside, covering most of the plywood exterior and the roof with metal.

Gail had worked with her father putting an addition on their family home, so she had confidence in her carpentry skills. She also read up on carpentry and house building at the library. I read about solar design, and drew plans for a southern exposure using passive solar technology inside.[1] There would be fixed windows with small vents, and plastic water storage barrels that absorb heat in summer and radiate heat out in winter to warm the house. Outside, we would have a wood-heated hot tub, a metal tub with concrete blocks and wood pallet floor. We both came up with ideas and got together on the design.

When we moved to the land, we were getting into all kinds of spirituality and had the idea we would be able to raise the walls with humming, like the Pyramids, maybe levitate the walls into place [laughter]. That didn't happen. "We raised them the old-fashioned way," Gail says. We began to build our house, Cedar Place, in 1982 using post and beam construction.

Georganne put the aluminum on the roof. We had a roof and a north wall and plastic when we moved in the next spring. During the spring and summer of 1984, we added windows that I had found and Gail's teacher friends had donated.

Georganne and Bluejay began to build a cabin named Dogwood in 1982, but Bluejay left after a few months. In the fall of that first year, Gail decided to get a job teaching in Holly Springs so we could afford a well. While we were out of town for Thanksgiving, Gail says, "The well man got in and dug the well [so] we're not sure how deep it is." When we returned, we ran pipes to the dome kitchen.

---

1 An article detailing our construction process is included in the book *Women Builders and Designers: Making Ourselves a Home,* by Janice Goldfrank (Watsonville, CA: Papier-Mache Press, 1995), 74–82.

In the spring of 1984, we started the bathhouse, with help from many women. We completed it with a ritual of our moon lodge women, sleeping with our heads together in a circle, January 1, 1987, in the bathhouse.

In August 1985, Pat and Annabel built a modified yurt, with straight walls and a cable around the outside to hold the roof up, so you didn't have to have a post in the middle. They hired Mr. Keel [from the nearby store] to do some carpentry finishing work for them on the bathhouse and the yurt. "That kind of got us some points with the neighbors," said Gail. Pat had some guys from her work come out and build the foundation. It's the only building on the land that has a concrete foundation built down into the land, just pilings in the ground. It's sturdy. A lot of women have lived in it since then. Annabel's dad was in construction and laid a nice gravel driveway for us.

In 1988, we installed a new shitter at Cedar Place and the first electric heated baths. In 1990, we built a barn with help from several women, and other women fenced and gated Cedar Place Garden. In the winter of 1991, we began the addition to our house [again with the help of other women], added insulation and siding in 1992, and in 1993, Ayla finished a greenhouse. In December of 1995, two Dutch women helped build a bathroom inside our house. In the early 2000s, Glenda and Sherry got jobs in the vicinity, brought out a double-wide trailer to live in, and made big improvements to our driveway. Now their trailer is for rent since they have moved to a nearby town for work.

In every project, through all the years, we made small improvements with the help of many, many women. We succeeded in creating an affordable home, being involved in the building process, and providing a place to share with other women.

Residents

Many women saw Silver Circle ads in *Lesbian Connection* and came to live on the land in tents or trailers or in the existing structures. Some women were apprentices; others were craftswomen and artists who needed a home for a few months before striking out on the festival circuit. Others stayed for a while to learn skills and to save money to buy their own land.

We met Ayla Heartsong the summer of 1988 at the annual WIT's End "Unfinished Revolution" party in July (see "WIT's End," p. 106). For a long time, Ayla would come for the winter, and go back to Wisconsin in the summer to farm with Trish. She has lived at Silver Circle off and on all these years in the Dogwood cabin. Our friendship with Ayla has grown through the years into a trusted partnership. Ayla organized a twenty-fifth-year anniversary party for us in 2007 at Silver Circle. It was a large gathering of friends from our church in Memphis, and elsewhere in Tennessee and Georgia.

Though not many women have lived on the land continuously, they help out and learn a lot while they're here. Many come back on a regular basis.

Philosophy

The country life always called to us both. Gail spent time on her grandmother's farm in Charleston, Tennessee. I had lived at Lone Star farm [a commune] outside of Memphis before partnering with Gail. I was always into communal living and gardening. I loved country living. Before Silver Circle, I learned gardening, enjoyed an abundance of crops, raised pigs, cows, and chickens. I knew raising animals was too much work, and I did not want to pen them up or to kill them for meat.

Both of us dreamed of living in a world like the Michigan festival where women created everything. We were determined to commit our money and energy to this effort. We wanted to live away from male energy. We thought communal living would produce an environment where women shared the workload, could live more cheaply, and have fun socializing. We wanted a place "where women could find out what they could be," Gail added.

We put ads in *Lesbian Connection*, and as contact dykes, we welcomed women to stay in exchange for work. We found that new jobs, love relationships, and money hardships often caused the women to move away after short periods. Ayla continues to live in Dogwood and maintains much of the repair work. We plan to leave the land to Glenda, Sherry, and Ayla, who will continue to nurture it. Now over thirty years later, Gail and I have many happy memories of all the women who shared their lives at Silver Circle for small snatches of time.

HARVESTING FROM *MAIZE*
Barbara Ester and Robin Toler

Lesbians who shared land in the Southern states wrote of their successes and challenges in *Maize, a Lesbian Country Magazine.* First published in New York in 1983, *Maize* has provided an open venue for Lesbians throughout the country—indeed throughout the world—to write about their journeys out of patriarchal influence and onto the land where it was assumed they could be free from the hands of the patriarchal constructs that constantly pushed up against these free-spirited women. Many women wrote about their newfound freedom and the costs—personal and emotional—of living in rural areas. They explored multidimensions related to their health, well-being, and safety. They longed for utopia, and they idealized their peers. Many did not foresee the issues and problems stemming from the internalized patriarchy they sought to leave behind. Their expectations were great.

Maize advertised in *Lesbian Connection*, at festivals, and in other Lesbian publications. Some Lesbians had access to or the privilege of owning their own land in the country. In the first issue, spring 1983, publisher Beverly Brown writes about the "foundation of rural values being built on genocide, slavery and indentured labor of people of color and poor whites" but also asserts, "We belong here, we are not urban by nature."[1] Questioning rural values would prompt deep soul-searching regarding established patriarchal, class, and social values among the Lesbians who were finding their way to these lands with the dream of creating communities. Decisions regarding moneymaking, via income-producing "jobs" in cities or urban areas, countered with those who were choosing

---

1 "The Lesbian Geography of Change," *Maize* 1 (1983): 28.

to create cottage industries using the skills they brought with them. One Lesbian writer suggests creating an "interdependent" community between country and city/urban wimmin, "financially, emotionally, spiritually and physically."[2]

Arco Iris, in Arkansas, was the first Southern land group to write about their land and "privilege." Miguela writes: "few women of color are ready to leave the city, . . . considered backward for many of us whose parent or grandparents only just moved to the cities 30 or 50 years ago, who just got running water and worked hard for a few comforts so recently earned."[3] Obtaining water and being self-sufficient, she states, are priorities "on the land."

They describe the terrain of their land, the acreage acquired, water and utility access, their gardens, building projects and the intent and focus of their communities. Lots of physical work is involved, and urban-raised wimmin are often not reliable or as skilled. Several wimmin suggest that "urban" wimmin are not as respectful to the land as those who grew up in the country. Finding others to join the communities, to stay on, is a common challenge. Lesbians on land in six Southern states search for others to join them. They offer workshops to learn farming, building, and survival skills. Marianne in North Carolina mentions the fear that "in rural areas where things are more traditional, especially in the South, it can be pretty rough if you are a known Lesbian."[4] Living in safety and protecting their lands is a significant concern for many.

Sustana, from Spinsterhaven (Arkansas), writes about not being able to attract new women to older established lands: "As one woman put it, 'I couldn't realize my own dream there. They don't really want to incorporate new ideas; they want wimmin who will help them accomplish what they have already planned.'"[5]

2 "Interdependence: A Survival Skill," *Maize* 7 (1986): 6.

3 "On the Land, Arco Iris," *Maize* 2 (1984): 26.

4 "Letters," *Maize* 5 (1985): 20.

5 "Participation in Paradise," *Maize* 54 (1997): 35.

And in the same piece, Sustana writes of women travelers: "I suspect that our understanding of the journeying wimmin is more important to the Landyke Community than any of us realize. It is these wimmin who provide the only constant human cohesiveness that exists in our community. The only other things we have are *Maize*, our newsletters, and the [Landyke] Gatherings, if they become annual events.[6] But I think most of us haven't even noticed that these wimmin could be forming a necessary, natural part of our community."[7]

Southern Lesbian Landykes supported *Maize*, and *Maize* supported Southern Lesbian Landykes—it was a reciprocal relationship—but it is clear that Lesbian nation is not defined by patriarchal boundaries. In Louisiana, Shewolf writes of what Myriam Fougère calls "Lesbiana": "Perhaps our Lesbian nation is worldwide geographically, even universal. Perhaps we form states within our nation related to environmental conditions. If our culture map spans Lesbians in the states of ruraldom, urbandom, and traveldom (mobiledom, itinerantdom, nomadom), then each state has its own feminine boundaries, which are fluid and not rigid as in the patriarchal world. We can feel attached to the larger whole of the Lesbian nation, the state we love, and move from state to state when our lives desire it."[8]

Maize continues to publish every season. The Lesbians who live on land in the Southern states are determined to keep their dreams alive. With the obvious challenges, there are many rewards of living in the country, having close interrelations with nature and to "experience a reality created by earth-conscious consensual living,"[9] to be with your friends, to learn better communication skills, and to truly be free to imagine and create a more peaceful way of living.

---

6   Landyke Gatherings have indeed continued. The thirteenth gathering was held in fall 2013 at We'Moon Land in Oregon.

7   "Participation in Paradise," *Maize* 54 (1997): 35.

8   "The Uniting States of the Lesbian Nation," *Maize* 54 (1997): 33.

9   "On the Land; Whypperwillow, Arkansas," *Maize* 6 (1985): 25.

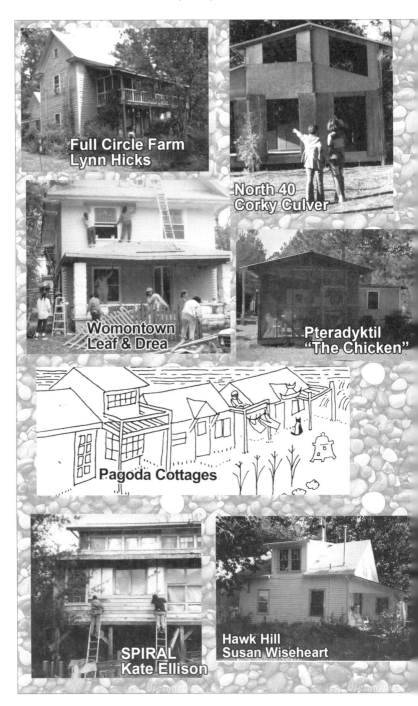

Full Circle Farm
Lynn Hicks

North 40
Corky Culver

Womontown
Leaf & Drea

Pteradyktil
"The Chicken"

Pagoda Cottages

SPIRAL
Kate Ellison

Hawk Hill
Susan Wiseheart

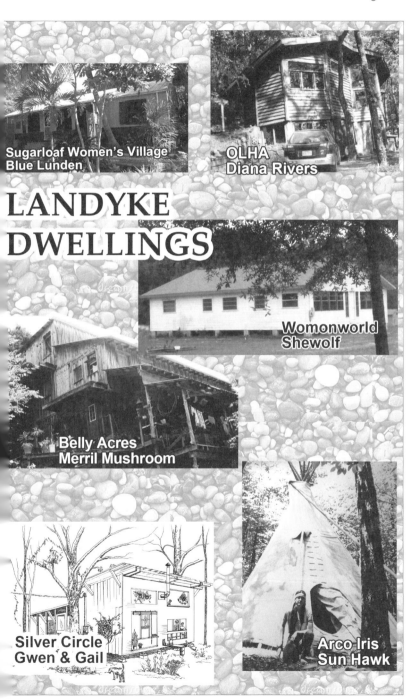

LANDYKE DWELLINGS

Sugarloaf Women's Village
Blue Lunden

OLHA
Diana Rivers

Womonworld
Shewolf

Belly Acres
Merril Mushroom

Silver Circle
Gwen & Gail

Arco Iris
Sun Hawk

Full Circle Farm - Photo courtesy of Lynn Hicks
North 40 - Photo by Pat Paul, courtesy of Corky Culver
Sugarloaf - Photo by Rose Norman
OLHA - Photo courtesy of Merril Mushroom
Womontown - Photo courtesy of B. Leaf Cronewrite
Pagoda - Drawing by Rainbow Williams, used with permission
Belly Acres - Photo courtesy of Merril Mushroom
Womonworld - Photo courtesy of Shewolf
Pteradyktil - Photo by Judy McVey
SPIRAL - Photo courtesy of Kate Ellison
Hawk Hill - Photo courtesy of Susan Wiseheart
Cedar Place at Silver Circle - Drawing by Gwen Demeter,
    used with permission
Arco Iris - Photo courtesy of Águila
Landyke dwellings collage by Suzanne Barbara

PTERADYKTIL: LESBIAN LAND AND CHANGE
Judy McVey

esbian land was not something I had ever thought about. I had only been out three years. In 1983, I was thirty-four years old and teaching music in Atlanta when I received money from an inheritance and decided to invest in land. As I began to involve my friends in the process, the land idea quickly evolved into shared Lesbian space, a safe place for us to camp on weekends, a place to be ourselves and share our lives and stories.

I chose east Georgia between Atlanta and Savannah for a rural location. After checking several small-town newspapers, my two housemates made an overnight trip in September to look at some advertised properties. They came back with several possibilities and an area map of the one they liked best. That night over dinner five of us discussed the various sale properties. I had to go to a meeting, and when I returned, the others were still there huddled over the seventy-two-acre property map. They had drawn little circles on it indicating where their cabins would be!

A few weeks later, I drove down with a friend and looked at all the properties. When I saw the seventy-two-acre lot, it was love at first sight! Two-thirds were wooded, with the rest open soybean fields. It was bordered by a creek, two branches, and a dirt road, and most was hidden from the road and neighbors. It was beautiful. My offer was accepted, and the paperwork was started. The owner offered to let me use the property in the meantime, so in October, five of us drove down for a beautiful camping weekend. On the way home, we named it "Pteradyktil," after the flying dinosaur Pterodactyl, as a play on words: terra-dyke-till. On Friday, November 18, the land was mine. Although it was in my name, I knew I wanted to share it with friends. Our first November weekend, we were a cluster of colorful tents around a campfire with a row of compact cars parked off to the side sporting alternative and political bumper stickers. Women friends from Atlanta, Athens, and Savannah shared a potluck dinner spread out on an old door supported by sawhorses. That afternoon several women presented to the land a large cast-iron dinner bell that now calls us to meals or campfire and s'mores.

In those early days, we had great times together picking up trash, hauling off broken appliances and scrap metal, laying water pipe, creating and naming trails, and cleaning out the old pig barn. When I had the electricity turned on, that barn became our kitchen. The third year, my carpenter friend moved to the land and held workshops for women that led to the building of the first small cabin. All of the measuring and sawing took place at the barn, and then materials were trucked to the site for construction. It was exciting to be part of a team of women raising a wall and nailing it into place! Over the next ten years, we added three more cabins, all with simple solar power systems.

We began organic farming in 1987, using "Sandhill Farms" as our marketing name. It required a lot of research and some serious

Photo courtesy of Judy McVey

start-up costs, including tractor implements and irrigation equipment. Only two organic markets existed at the time, so produce had to be trucked two to three hours away each week in opposite directions. My resident friend did most of the planning and work, and several of us came down different weekends to help as our own jobs permitted. Each summer, we had an intern living in one of the cabins

Judy McVey with Vidalia onions in her organic garden.

to help, but the work was labor intensive, and we were not able to break even. After three years, we gave it up.

Paula Winter with organic produce at Pteradyktil (Sandhill Farm).

We continued to spend frequent weekends on the land, some of them large group celebrations with as many as thirty women attending. At times, various women lived here in a tent or one of the cabins for several months to a year. There were safety concerns, as often the land was unattended. Visitors were cautioned to be clothed if they were on that part of the property visible from the road and were asked to maintain a low profile while in town. We worked to create good relations with our neighbors, who mostly were conservative, small-scale farmers.

After the first four to five years, the old familiar issues came up: women-only space, boy children, money, power struggles, and spirituality, to name a few. There was endless processing. Around this time, several friends moved to another state, some stopped coming after disagreements, and several couples broke up. By 1992, no one was living here, so I hired a local handyman to handle the mowing, tractor care, and repairs as needed. He was very capable and was comfortable with us as Lesbians. It was a major shift for us to have a man on the land so much of the time. Then some of our gay male friends began coming down, as well as the Lesbians and straight women. Several gay-friendly religious groups have retreats here, as many have found it to be a spiritual place, a place of quiet and healing. My best friend adopted a twenty-seven-month-old girl in 1996, and soon other mothers with children were coming for weekends and vacation. None of this was planned! The land was a great place for children to run, explore the many trails, and gain some independence from their moms.

Many kids have learned to swim here as we have progressed from wading pool to above ground to finally an in-ground pool. By 1997, the mice were winning the battle for our kitchen in the barn, so I had a prefab building delivered. Our handyman added electricity, cabinets and countertops, a bathroom, a screened porch, and an outdoor shower. We finally had a comfortable climate-controlled place where we could gather, have meetings and meals, or just hang out and play games. One of our children could not say "kitchen," and said "chicken" instead. How appropriate for a farm! We have called it "the Chicken" ever since.

When I retired from teaching in 2000, my partner and I sold our Atlanta house and moved to the farm. We put in a double-wide manufactured home at one end of the property and the in-ground pool at the other end, closer to cabins, campsite, and the Chicken. The next year a gay male friend moved into a cabin on the property and lived here with us for twelve years. His three children visited every few weeks, so they have practically grown up here. Family members, including two grandchildren, have joined us over the years for many visits. A Lesbian friend moved into one of the cabins in 2008 and has been a great help around the place. We have been able to connect with the local gay folks with some success, mostly through potlucks and small celebrations. Two gay campgrounds are a couple of hours from us and occasionally have

Lesbian weekends, so we sometimes meet there. Most of our close friends are still those we have in Atlanta. Times have changed, and we now feel safer here as people have come to know us, but we are discriminating about coming out.

We continue to see change as we grow older and our friends are able to drive here less often. The trip is more difficult, some have moved farther away, gas is expensive, and the children are grown, leaving them with more time for adult activities closer to home. They are dealing with their own life changes. We still are Lesbians on land, but perhaps this is no longer just Lesbian land. Pteradyktil has become more open in ways we never could have imagined or planned. This November we will celebrate thirty-two years at Pteradyktil.

WIT'S END FARM

Mary Bricker-Jenkins

**WIT: Women in Transition/World in Transformation . . .
or "Where you go when you're already there" (1984–2014)**

In 1984, I was smitten. Teaching at CNR;[1] summering at Camp Thoreau. Ran the Liberation Laundromat. C transferred from UN[2] to Int'l Fertilizer Development Center. Call to camp offering one year at MTSU.[3] Left everything for love, which lasted two weeks.

Decided to have a fling. Met Merril. Climbed the mountain (OK, the hill), saw the land over the ridge, decided I needed to stay in the South and become a Landyke. Began search for the land the next day. "Old Vandergriff farm for sale. . ." It was the land I had seen from the ridge. Land grant to Vandergriffs, Mae and Floyd. Made offer to Miss Mae; turned down.

Kept looking. Always back to Vandergriff farm. "That's not a good place. No water." Overgrown with blackberries and multiflora rose. Not much bottom; steep, rocky hills. But something drew me, the women's land in the back. Gnarled cedars at entrance, pathway cool and soft up to a wall of blackberry bushes protecting a once-cultivated field and pretty pond.

Tried "everything" to get Miss Mae to accept, including counteroffer by my own sister (long story). At end of summer, leaving for NY, asked once more. Miss Mae said no (with regret). Stopped by Okra Ridge. Catherine Risingflame teaches "words of power." I do that.

Months later, visiting Merril. Paid visit to Miss Mae, just to say hello. Floyd appears. "Who's that?". . . "Lady that wanted to

1 College of New Rochelle.
2 United Nations
3 Middle Tennessee State University.

buy the farm." "They say there was a witch lived back there by the Eliac Field. I used to have corn. One day I was plowing back there, turned up some old pots. Decided I wasn't going to plant back there anymore. There was a burning. . ." Miss Mae said it was foolish talk.

She called me the next morning. "I decided that you're supposed to have the land, Mairee. I accept your price." Her children had objected. She'd "take care of that."

. . .

Visits to Eliac Field, still difficult to access through wall of blackberries and thorny bushes, but "Cora" was there. The spirit. The ghost. The witch. The ritual—with Merril—and a man friend, of all things! (student of Kabbalah). Told Cora she was safe now. During the winter, all the thorny trees and brush died back. Harvesting mullein, discovered the birthing tree. Better understood what "women's land" meant.

. . .

Peter, David, J'aime. Snowy day. Discovery of the blowhole to a cave.

. . .

Gatherings, especially Unfinished Revolution. Fancy dinner parties. Writing, including dissertation with invocation to four corners. Myths and legends in the community, including tall naked woman on the porch with a rifle. Always open to women in transition. Known only by word of mouth; necessary to preserve the skill so we can find each other when the time comes.

. . .

Cancer, 1988. Clearing the land of multiflora rose (introduced by government in 1950s as natural fence, but didn't belong and took over). Visualizing clearing body of invasive, foreign matter. Another transformation: birth of Multiflora Rose, the Lesbian madam. Bringer of health.

SEARCHING FOR THE DREAM:
GATHERING ROOT FARM, 1985–2011

Jenna Weston

"It's not so much a house
That I miss
Or even a particular location;
What I crave is some earth—
Connection that is not transitory."
　　Jennifer Weston, *Maize* 2 (1984): 8

It wasn't going to be just any road trip. My partner Jo and I were setting off cross-country determined to find a piece of Lesbian Land to call our home. It was 1984, that watershed year when Ronald Reagan got reelected, and clearly things weren't going to be like the Seventies anymore. It seemed to be a good time to leave the city and go back to living simply and self-sufficiently in the country. We needed a safe place to dig in for the backlash we felt was coming against the gains we had made as women and Lesbians in the Seventies. Our intention was to buy a farm and create a place where other Lesbians would come join us. There we would live together—building cabins, growing our own food, and sharing the work and the joy of a woman-only commune—far from the Patriarchy.

First we had to outfit our empty panel van so that we could live in it for an undetermined length of time as we traveled the country on our search. We got a dyke carpenter to build us a bed, storage spaces, and a makeshift kitchen. Jo had sold her house, and I had just inherited a small sum from my father's death. We put all our money in the bank and lived off the interest for the next two years, never touching the principal. It was not that much money, but interest rates back then could be as high as twenty percent, and our only real expenses were food, gas, vehicle insurance, and repairs. We had joined the ranks of what was unofficially known as The Van Dykes.[1]

Jo and I had been living together for six years in Grand Rapids, Michigan. We were both deeply involved in Aradia, the women's organization and community there. It was not easy to leave our close family of friends, but the dream of the land was calling to us. I had grown up on a farm, and Jo was a proficient gardener, so we thought we had some idea of what we were getting into. Our plan was to drive from women's land to women's land all across the continental United States, until we recognized a special place where we were destined to put down our roots.

We visited dozens of women's lands, staying at some for months. Circling the country twice, we somehow kept ending up in the southern Missouri Ozarks. Land was incredibly cheap there, and it was reputed to be one of the least polluted areas in the entire country. We found eighty beautiful acres of woods, hills, fenced pastures, ponds, and an organic garden, with a big old farmhouse and barn. A year-round crystal-clear creek flowed through the middle of it, and at night the stars were brilliant against a very dark sky. There weren't any signs of other human habitation to be seen from this land, and the only sounds seemed to be the wind in the trees and birdsong. With $42,000 from our combined savings, we could "buy" all this. We figured we had found Paradise.

And for a while it seemed so. I was an artist and had learned to make baskets so was able to bring in some money selling at craft shows. Jo was an accountant, and picked up some tax jobs in the area. With no mortgage to pay, and by growing a fair amount of our own food, we didn't need a lot of money. We worked our tails off fixing up the old house and stewarding the land, but we were in our thirties, so had lots of energy. I began to bond with this land in a primal way.

---

1 In 2009, *The New Yorker* published an article about Van Dykes, but Jo and I were not "members" of that group and never even met any of them. We had just somehow heard about them and thought that was a cool name. See Ariel Levy's "Lesbian Nation: Why Gay Women Took to the Road," *The New Yorker*, March 22, 2009, online at http://www.newyorker.com/reporting/2009/03/02/090302fa_fact_levy

I discovered portraits of myself in the landscape. The limestone rocks and cliffs became part of a new backbone. The scaffolding of trees was the ribs that protected my unfurling heart. And the creek flowed through the channels of my veins.

Drawing by Jenna Weston, used with her permission

Lesbians in Their Garden.

In the first years, there was a nonstop stream of Lesbian visitors to the land we had named Gathering Root Farm. However, none of those women were interested in actually moving onto the land with us. We hadn't counted on what a drawback it was to be twenty-five miles from the nearest town of 2000 people. The closest city where we could go to a movie, art museum, or store of any size was ninety miles away, much of it via winding back roads. Of course, local jobs were practically nonexistent, so that eliminated anyone who needed to earn money in conventional ways. The internet had not come into use yet, and even when it did later, we could only get painfully slow dial-up service.

The things that made our land so unpolluted and quiet also meant that we were pretty darned isolated. For a few years, it was a twenty-five- to thirty-mile drive to where the nearest Lesbians lived. Then some dyke friends from Michigan settled onto a land trust just four miles away, Hawk Hill [see story, p. 130]. Later, a couple of other Lesbians bought into that land trust as well. So we had a small, insular community within a dominant culture that was alien to us, primarily white heterosexual people with extremely conservative political and religious views, who had lived in those hills for generations.

Around that time, I was knocked unconscious by my horse, temporarily losing my short-term memory. That seemed to have the effect of literally jarring loose some intense repressed emotions still lurking in my brain from childhood abuse. Subsequently, I went into a protracted and very deep depression. There was very little understanding of, or support for, any kind of mental illness in that rural area, so we had to cope as best we could. What I had not realized when leaving our Aradian community in Michigan was that we were giving up a strong safety net of resources and the support of many other women. The pressure of having to be everything for each other became too much for us. My partner was no longer able to handle my inability to function normally. We split up the farm, with me getting the house and land around it, and she getting the cabin and the rest of the land. I had to leave and go to a city for a while to find a support group where I could heal. When I came back to the land, I was determined to carry on the dream.

I was certain that I would never leave this place. When I died I would be buried under the huge dogwood in the upper pasture. Particles of my horse's bones scurried around inside generations of field mice who had gnawed on her carcass after I had had to put her

*down in the woods. The pond watched over my days with its single
eye. What I grew and ate from the garden became me. Although I
attempted to shape the land, the truth was, the land shaped me
much more. I was not aware that this sculpting was subtly distorting
my form.*

I faced some hard years of trying to run a small farm on my
own with very little income. I took any job available in the area to
supplement my erratic art studio income, from caring for a sick
woman to being a house cleaner. During this time, I periodically
rented out half the farmhouse to other women, while I lived in the
other half. The old house and barn needed major repairs I could
not afford. As I aged, the area I was able to garden grew smaller
every year.

*I no longer felt that I was living in my natural habitat. I had not
simply reached some fork in the road, but an unequivocal dead end.
Like a root-bound plant, I was not able to grow another inch in my
once-beloved container. I needed to transplant myself.*

It became clear to me that I had to be somewhere less difficult
and isolated, somewhere I could get involved as a member of a
larger women's community. The idea of putting the farm up for
sale was excruciating, as was finally letting go of the dream of
creating a women's community there.

Somehow I summoned the wherewithal to move on—and I
found my new life partner in the process! Eventually, we settled in
a place that I feel at home in now. Being a part of the Gainesville,
Florida, women's community is so reminiscent of the years I was
a part of Aradia in Michigan. Perhaps the dream was waiting for
when I was finally ready. It seems I have come full circle. Along the
way, I learned some hard lessons and gained a lot of experience
from living as a Landyke for a quarter of a century. I guess that has
all contributed to shaping me into the tougher and wiser crone I
am today.

SHE PUT LANDYKES ON THE MAP:
SHEWOLF'S DIRECTORY

Kate Ellison

S ince 1993, Shewolf (Dr. Jean Boudreaux) has published six editions of *Shewolf's Directory of Wimmin's Lands and Lesbian Communities*, on average one every three years.[1] Shewolf made her way around the country from her home base in Louisiana to visit as many Lesbian lands as possible. While most of the groups listed are located in the United States, a few are scattered around the English-speaking world, plus a few European countries. I interviewed her in August 2014.

What do you think is the significance or value of the Directory?

It was a miracle it happened at all. I believe it was important to document this movement, to show how widespread it was, and to give these women a way to find each other. I lived in my own land community, Womonworld, and knew firsthand how hard it was for us to connect.

I developed a questionnaire to gather the basic information, with a long blank space for whatever they wanted to say. I had to push most of the women to figure out a way to put information in, even if they didn't feel safe revealing where they were. Many were hidden or not looking for new members. I would write up the entries, and add my comments if I had visited them. The first few editions were advertised through *Maize* and *Lesbian Connection*,

---

1 The title of the first directory says "1994-1995," but it was actually published in 1993. All of the *Shewolf Directories* were published the year before the first year in the title. To order *Shewolf's Directory* (6ᵗʰ ed.), send $16.00 ppd in USA funds to P.O. Box 1515, Melrose, FL 32666, for one copy delivered to any USA address. On check or money order, on "Pay to" line, write JRB, nothing else. For orders to be delivered outside the USA, the cost is $25.00, including postage. If you have questions after reading the *Directory*, write to Shewolf at Wimminland@aol.com.

and sold at festivals and a few women's bookstores—only marketed to Lesbians, in other words. The fifth edition, 2007, was the first to be sold over the internet, on my own website set up for that purpose.

The *Directory* balances on that edge between safety and privacy on one side, publicity and outreach on the other. Some wouldn't put their information in if it said "Lesbian" on the cover; I took the 'L' word off for the second edition and didn't put it back till 2007 (fifth edition). There was a lot of fear in the beginning, even though it was the 1990s. Women living rurally were very secretive at first, and many would not let me publish their contact information. I kept publishing what they allowed, though, and no trouble came to the communities, so they gradually became more open.

Will you publish another one?

I would like to, but in reality, I'm looking for someone else to carry it forward. I've kept the names and addresses of everyone who has ordered it, and of course the contact information (not published) for each land group. For the first time, with the current edition, it is paying for itself. All editions were self-published, and I did all the work, except for two years when a gal in New Orleans handled the orders and mailings. Now, the *Directory* sells itself— more and more women want one. Three or four times a month I get thank-you notes, many saying they found their new home on Lesbian land through the *Directory*. This edition will be sold out soon. I'm already getting requests to be listed in the next edition. What a difference from that first secretive edition!

SHEWOLF'S WOMONWORLD,[1]
SOUTH LOUISIANA

B. Leaf Cronewrite

"Women who aren't afraid of hard work, living without luxury, and stretching themselves emotionally to learn to be real and loving, are encouraged to write and tell me their dreams. As we make a match, this community will be off and operating, before the end of 1990!" Shewolf, "Woman's World," Madisonville, Louisiana, Maize 24 (1990): 11

On February 19, 2013, Barbara Esrig interviewed Shewolf in her home in Melrose, Florida. From that 6000-word interview, B. Leaf Cronewrite excerpted the following passages about Shewolf's women's land experience in Louisiana and around the country.

BE: Were you drawn to going back to the land, living simply?
Shewolf: Yeah, my dad had a hundred acres in south Louisiana, and when I was a kid, I would go out there with him. Living in cities all my life, I saw that the land was something wonderful. And when I was thinking about retiring, I could see myself there.

Well, it must have been back in the 1960s, my dad retired. He really couldn't afford to retire, so he said, "I'm going to sell this land." And I said, "Okay, sell it to me." For twenty years, I paid my mother and dad for this land, and when I retired, I owned it!

BE: When did you start going there?
Shewolf: The farm was in my family, and I started buying it from my father in 1969. Roughly. I was teaching at [the University of Louisiana] Lafayette, and it was about a hundred miles to the

---

1 Shewolf called the land Woman's World in *Maize* articles, but today prefers Womonworld.

land. It was paid off when I retired in 1985, when I started working on creating community there.

BE: How many buildings did you have?

Shewolf: There was a house, an old Jim Walter house that my dad had started for my brother and his wife before they decided they didn't want to live there. It never got finished, but my whole family had worked on it. The land, this house, and the barn, that was it.

We started off by going to the dairy and getting these little four-week-old calves. [My girlfriend] Sandy and I bottle-fed them for six weeks or so until they got on grain. When they were big enough, three, four months old, they were ready for slaughter. So we took them to the slaughterhouse, and they gave us back these boxes of frozen steaks. We took them home, and we put them on the table, and we couldn't eat them. We just couldn't eat them. I don't know what we did. We gave it all away or something, but we never did eat the damn things.

We raised Black Angus for about six years, for breeding. But we ended up with a bunch of baby Black Angus bulls. Two agriculture agents came out and looked at my herd, and they liked them. Because I had some really good stock. So what I ended up doing was selling them to the local agricultural agents. So I really never slaughtered any more of my cattle.

BE: How many women eventually lived on the land?

Shewolf: Well, that was like a fruit basket turnover. I did carpentry, so I got into teaching workshops on basic carpentry. The ads said "for women," but it was teaching Lesbians. The idea was, they would come and learn basic skills to take back to their land, and they would build their own little cabins. It was easier to build a little cabin if you already had outdoor toilets and you had running water and all. Well, I had workshops, about four or five a year, for about twelve years. And the women would come to the land and live for a while. They would live in the woods, set up a kitchen . . . and whatever they needed. And we would teach them.

I had a couple gals who would help me teach sometimes. The idea was that women would come and some would stay, while some would go back home and build on their land.

Shewolf on tractor at Womonworld, 1980s.

You know the old routine. They'd come, they'd eat, they'd sleep, they'd do the building workshops, . . . and I was paying for the food and materials most of the time. I used up about $50,000 just having workshops because people couldn't pay to come to them. They would just come. Several women came and lived on the land because they had an RV or camper, and a couple gals signed up for two years. What I was trying to do was portion off some of the land so that women would have two or three acres to live on forever. But it never really worked out. They all had reasons for coming and reasons for leaving. Each one was different. Most of the women who came were pretty nice gals who did a good job, but they had issues. They all had issues.

Womonworld started out being a Landyke place where Lesbians could come and live, but it turned into a workshop place where they came and learned skills and left. And after a while, I gave up trying to make it into anything else. They would come for one or two or three weeks and then they'd go. For example, three gals came one time and the four of us built a yurt on top of a platform. One would teach belly dancing; another cooked like a dream. She cooked all these healthy foods—I ate tofu for the first time when she came and cooked for us. The four of us had three weeks of joy.

Photo courtesy of Shewolf

Shewolf fencing after the storm at Womonworld in 1978.

BE: But nobody really stayed long enough that you could say you were creating community there?

Shewolf: Yes and no. We had three gals who stayed long enough to have a community, but about the time where you would start having the problems of community, the infighting and all, they were on their way out. And, I think a lot of people were afraid of the South, afraid to come to Louisiana. Unfounded fears. I mean, the first thing you'd hear from people when you'd write was, "Do you have alligators?" There were more snakes than there were alligators. It was really unrealistic.

There isn't a community out there that doesn't have its problems. When I was visiting all the lands, I always sat in on their community meetings. I would listen to all the dialogue, and the thing was, I never carried tales from one to the next. They knew I wasn't going to criticize them. I wasn't going to take sides or try to influence them in any way, and so I got to hear a lot.

BE: Did you come to any conclusions about why it has been so difficult? Why conflicts come?

Shewolf: Well, yeah. When I first started out looking at lands, and started trying to make a unity at Womonworld, my little wise friend in California who was about ten years younger than I was, she looked me in the eye and she said, you are not going to get five Lesbians who want to do the same thing at the same time in the same way. Forget it! And I ignored it for twenty years, but she was right. Everybody has the feeling that if you build it they will come. T'ain't true.

Bleeding the diesel tractor when dry,
Charrean at Womonworld, 1980.

Everybody has the feeling that they know how they want it. They want vegetarian. They want to grow their own foods. They want to be healthy. They want to live on the land. They want to get off the grid. They want to have a feminist group. They want to cut themselves off from the mainstream. They want to be anti-male. They want to be pure, and they want to do this without any money. The women who are the most dedicated to doing this never ever had any money. The few who had money went out and bought their own land. They set up their own place and they said, "Y'all come." Nobody came, at least not for long. And it's the same all over.

I had seventeen good years at Womonworld. I still hear from women who were there, who learned something and went out and built things, and then they made crews and some traveled around. We had some great times.

TALES OF A TRAVELING DYKE

Naj McFadden

From December 1983 to July 1986, I traveled the United States staying exclusively with women or on women's land, trying to find the ideal place to live the rest of my life. I prepared for the trip for ten years, saving money and compiling a list of what would make a place ideal for me and how I would deal with any problems I might encounter. I sent out self-addressed stamped envelopes to all the Contact Dykes in *Lesbian Connection* in areas where I thought I might like to live, with a letter offering to do work in exchange for room and board and/or money, when possible. I was an electronics technician by trade and had experience in auto mechanics and the building trades.

I started in the upper Midwest, traveled through the upper South, and swung east through West Virginia. I headed south to North Carolina and then south along the coast, zigzagging inland at various places. I went all through Florida, then west all the way to San Diego. I traveled up the coast to Seattle, and returned to Indiana through the northern route.

Cold weather seemed to follow me. It was somewhere in the Mississippi Delta where I was staying with a woman who lived in an old sharecroppers cabin. It snowed so much that for five days we were unable to push the door open to get out. The only heat was the oven. I was able to repair a space heater and used old newspapers to insulate all the cracks in the walls. We wore all the clothes we could fit into and slept together on the kitchen table. I truly believe if I had not been there, she might have frozen to death.

When I was in Atlanta, there was a huge ice storm that shut the city down. Once it thawed, pipes burst all over the city and flooding was a problem. Since I was a Northerner, frozen pipes were something I was familiar with, so I was able to thaw out my host's (Liz Hill) pipes without any leaks or breaks.

In West Virginia, there were two women who owned a shop where they sold and repaired lawn maintenance equipment. The building had two bathrooms (men's and women's), and since they were all women, they wanted to turn one of the bathrooms into a shower and toilet. That was probably the most complicated job I did. I was careful about measuring so that the shower surround I would purchase would fit the space. What I failed to take into account was the size of the door. The shower would not fit through it. I had to knock out part of the connecting wall to angle the tub surround into place and then repair the wall. But I must say, I think the bathroom turned out nice.

I headed down the East Coast, detouring to visit Ladyslipper in Durham, North Carolina. Some of the women who worked there invited me to the coast for a long weekend where we all got horribly sunburned. One woman said she had heard toothpaste would help the burns, so we all smeared ourselves. I heard one woman had to go to the hospital after that weekend. I know it was several weeks before I could lie down comfortably.

I am not sure where I first met Myriam and Martine, two women from Canada who were also traveling. We kept running into each other all through Florida and were able to share information about Women's Land we had encountered and what women were doing various places. I felt a real kinship with them. It was like we were the equivalent of a traveling Lesbian newspaper, gathering and dispersing news throughout the South.

While in Florida, I heard about The North Forty in Melrose (see "The North Forty," p. 19) and attended the first LEAP conference. That was a real highlight for me and very energizing. It was very exciting meeting so many dynamic lesbians and learning about all the organizing that was going on. I was quite impressed with the community in and around Gainesville. It was at LEAP (October 19–21, 1984) that Judy McVey and I met working security together.

She invited me to her land, Sandhill, in Georgia (see "Pteradyktil," p. 101), and I ended up spending several months there, both during and after my trip. At that time, the land was a collective made up of Atlanta women, including Judy, Sandra Lambert, who worked at Charis Bookstore, a few other women, and Margaret Waters, who lived on the land in a solar-powered house she had designed and built. I worked on the solar wiring for Judy's house. I also put in an RV water heater in the barn, so we no longer had to boil water to do dishes or clean up, and built an enclosed outside shower. I valued my creature comforts!

I spent time at the Pagoda, a very magical place. I did a fair amount of electrical work there, but the only thing I recall was installing an outside light on the common building. I stayed at Sugarloaf Key, where Blue was living. We were old friends from our New York City days a decade before. It was summer time, and I was repairing and painting a ceiling in one of the guesthouses.

In northern Mississippi, I spent time with Gwen and Gail at Silver Circle, and helped them build a summer kitchen.

I stayed in New Orleans for several months because my $500 car needed to be replaced. I had lots of paying work doing odd jobs for Lesbian home owners. I also rewired a house for two women.

That about does it for my Southern adventures. I visited other Lesbian lands: Owl Farm and Jean Mountaingrove in Oregon; Outland in New Mexico, and Nett Hart and Lee Lanning's land in Minnesota, to name a few.

I stayed with 125 different Lesbians or land groups. One thing that became clear to me was the problem of ownership. If the land was privately owned, it was difficult, if not impossible, to form lasting community. The lands that still exist seem to be jointly owned or in land trusts of some type. And even many of those lands have fallen apart or have just one or two women living on them.

If any readers met me on my travels, I would love to reconnect with you. Email me at najtuna@yahoo.com and put LESBIAN in the subject line.

FULL CIRCLE FARM (1988—PRESENT)

Lynn Hicks

When I started farming, I came about it kind of by accident. I had been living in New York and Massachusetts for ten years in my twenties and thirties (the 1970s). In Massachusetts, I was living in an old farmhouse that a group of us had rented, and I started gardening for the first time. That was my first experience with any kind of community. We were gardening (not farming), and had a killing frost in August and never saw a ripe tomato! That influenced me to head back South for a longer growing season. I couldn't quite make it all the way back to Alabama, where I grew up, and anyway the growing season in North Carolina is better than in Alabama. That's what brought me to the Raleigh–Durham–Chapel Hill area, plus knowing there was a good progressive political climate here.

After I started farming, it came to me that it must be in my blood, and I began questioning my father about farming. His family had been farmers around Columbus, Georgia, for many generations. Just poor dirt farmers, not anything big. My father became the responsible person on the farm when he was very young, just starting out, and using a mule. When one farmer in the community got a tractor early on, maybe the 1920s, the whole community used that tractor. My father really took to it. He started tinkering with it and working on it, and became a mechanic that way. So after they lost the farm during the Depression, he got a job as a tractor mechanic, and worked with tractors the rest of his life.

When I got to North Carolina, I looked for people who wanted to live in the country and garden. I just wanted to rent some old house in the country and have a garden. There was a woman where I worked who was farming with her partner. She suggested I apprentice with them. So I lived and worked with them to learn farming. It had never occurred to me that you could actually make a living doing this. I just wanted to garden. But I decided to do that, and that was how I got introduced to farming.

I'm talking about market gardening, growing vegetables for farmers markets. By then I was raring to do it, and met a woman who had some land. I moved onto her land, and we got involved (that wasn't part of the plan, but it's what happened). So that was my first attempt at a Lesbian land community. Our fantasy at that time was to have women join us and create a community that had a cottage industry of farming. We invited other women to come and build out there, live out there, and farm. We were at it about five years. Another woman had come and built a house, and another couple was there. Each year, I had apprentices. What happened was that my partner and my apprentice got involved in a relationship with each other, and that blew the whole thing out of the water. I left, and the following year, she sold it and paid me my share. That gave me some money for a down payment when I bought my next farm in 1988, what became Full Circle Farm. I also had a small inheritance from my parents' death, from the sale of their house, and by then I was in a new relationship, with Yahoo, also called Marilyn.

Marilyn/Yahoo had a job and could get a mortgage, and I had about $30,000 from the sale of that other farm and from what I inherited from my parents. I put it all into a down payment on the farm. I call it the Last Great Land Deal.

We were just a couple with a hundred acres we wanted to share. It was during the late 1980s and 1990s, when there were lots of women looking, traveling through, staying anywhere from three months to a year. There was a big, old, unmortgageable farmhouse on the land, and we were living in it together. Our fantasy was that the farmhouse would be a community house and we would all build little shelters, little personal spaces, but still share the big farmhouse.

Four years after we bought Full Circle Farm, Yahoo suddenly died in a mountain climbing accident. Though brokenhearted, I was lucky enough to inherit her share (and the mortgage) without issues from her family. I did have to pay estate taxes on the inheritance. She worked for the state as an environmentalist and had some death benefits that I used to pay off the land loan. I had thought I was going to lose the farm, since she was the one paying it off. In the end, she did pay off the loan.

We had always wanted to keep the land intact and have a land trust or some entity to own the land instead of individuals. One of the problems with doing that was that the women who wanted to own that way had no money, and I couldn't give the land to a land trust. Women needed to buy a share, so the women who wanted to own that way didn't have money, and women who did have money needed the security of having a piece of paper for their investment. For a while, it went with just women being there temporarily, from three months to a year. After a year's trial period, they would leave because they couldn't buy in. A few stayed and rented or did work exchange.

I had about given up on having a Lesbian land community when a series of events led me to what is now a Lesbian land group. It was quite by accident, a serendipitous accident. In 2000, I had cancer. Even though I owned a hundred acres, I had no money. I had health insurance, but it had a high deductible, and I didn't have the money to pay my out-of-pocket expenses. Two of the women who had been there for a year in 1996, women from Florida (now in Tampa, Beth and Doreen), left because it was too cold for them, but they had wanted to just buy five acres from me and make community that way. In 2000, I needed some money, and the only thing I could do was sell land. I called them up and asked, "Do you still want to buy five acres from me?" (that's all I needed to sell). They almost immediately came up to North Carolina, and we started talking about community and what we could do with it. They ended up buying forty acres of Full Circle Farm. They were financially able to do surveys, pull power, and build roads to develop this little community of seven lots. We advertised in *LC*, in our local newsletter, and in *Maize*. All seven lots sold within about a year and a half.

Full Circle Farm resident Doreen Donovan.

The way Full Circle exists now, it is a community. We each own a piece of land, build our own houses, are very independent of each other, but share a lot. We own a tractor together, and a truck and tools. We share the maintenance, have work parties.

All those years, I had been trying to create a community where we all owned the land together, and it didn't work, but this did. Now all of those women who bought lots haven't built, and one couple decided not to move from Michigan, so sold theirs back. We have three houses on the land, plus a tree house. We have diversity in ages: the oldest are 68 and 70, two are in their forties, and they have two precious little girls (ages 6 and 10) who were born here, and the donor dad is a gay guy whose land backs up to ours. We have an acupuncturist, a nurse practitioner, and a psych nurse who live here! Of those who don't live here full-time, the youngest one is in her thirties, and others are in their forties or early fifties.

Of course, we have no (legal) control over who buys the lots, and we knew that from the beginning. So we have our legal covenants, which are mostly about the environment and nonviolence. And then we have a separate set of agreements, because you can't legally only have Lesbians. You hope that if somebody buys with that agreement, they agree with it. And if something happens and they don't, as has happened in other communities, we'll approach the buyers and say, "You know, we're all Lesbians," and hope we scare them away.

Right now, everybody is happy with it. We all act like we own it all. We ignore property lines, we ignore doors. We just walk into each other's houses, whether it's to borrow something or have coffee. So we all have the same feeling about it. We all own it all. I'm no longer farming, but we would really like for farmers to be here. Everybody has agreed that anybody who wants to farm can use any of the field land, regardless of who owns it.

Money and capitalism have not been a priority here (so far). When I sold the land, one of the things I said I would do (since I

Full Circle Farm landowners and friends, 2008.

Photo courtesy of Lynn Hicks and Doreen Donovan

wasn't going to invest the money in the stock market) was finance women who could not get a loan to buy land, which I did. I also sold it below market in order to make it more affordable. Land is expensive here, so still not as affordable as lands that are more remote.

We love to have visitors. Anyone who comes to visit usually stays at my house, because I live in the big old farmhouse. There's plenty of room there. We don't ask for any money, but most everybody leaves something. We share meals and try to get everyone together for a potluck. I love showing them around, the land and the area, a wonderful larger community.

We have a website: http://www.fullcirclefarms.htmlplanet. com/ and are on Facebook: Full Circle Farms.

For information about buying into Full Circle Farms Lesbian Neighborhood (30 minutes southwest of Chapel Hill, North Carolina), email LCLiving@aol.com. To arrange a visit, call Lynn at 919-742-5959 or email slhicks@embarqmail.com

HAWK HILL COMMUNITY LAND TRUST
Susan Wiseheart

In September 1989, I moved to the Missouri Ozarks after years of longing to live in the country, sparked by summers between ages two and fourteen spent on a small Indiana lake on what was once Potawatomi land, where I spent ecstatic summer weeks.

Hawk Hill Community Land Trust, where I still live, was "up for grabs," according to some Lesbians who lived near and were my dear friends, Jo Olszewski and Jenna Weston. It was while visiting them from our home in Grand Rapids, Michigan, that my then partner Terri and I were urged, the second time they took us to see Hawk Hill, to move here.

On the way home, we wrote a proposal to the board of the regional land trust (Ozark Regional Land Trust) that owns the land, which is to be held in trust in perpetuity and cared for assiduously. We were prepared to take on the conditions required: all organic growing, only sustainable forestry, if any, no row crops, no junkyards, no flush toilets (composting was "the way" among many of the back-to-the-land crowd already here for over a decade), and more.

We envisioned keeping a few farm animals and holding retreats for women artists and writers. There were a couple of very small artist retreats, but the idea never really took off, despite a lot of work being done on it, although we did have some workshops on topics like Permaculture. We knew very little about what was possible here in the Ozarks, and we were not really prepared for living twenty-two miles from the nearest town, but our proposal was accepted.

Partly that was due to Suzanne Pharr having given a workshop that a lot of the women around here attended, Lesbian, straight, and bi, and she had spelled out homophobia to them so clearly they immediately understood when some of the men on the board balked at Lesbians coming to live at Hawk Hill. Not for long. As I heard it described, one of the respected straight women "stamped her little foot," and the men eventually gave in. We would have a women's land trust and by that, we meant Lesbian.

Before a month was out, we were joined by another pair of friends who were passing through on their way to California, Denslow Brown and Linda Smith. They ended up staying, taking out their own lease, building a shed and then a house and eventually a donkey barn and a big storage barn. They're still here.

Linda Smith and Denslow Brown at Hawk Hill, 2009.

Terri and I took on the old farmhouse, now over a hundred years old and still doing well, built with materials from the very land on which we lived, my sweet little home where I have lived much longer than any other house in my life. We paid for a building with the same dimensions (24 × 24) built right next door to serve as Terri's art studio and my office, and we found ourselves caretakers of several other outbuildings. Before long, Lorraine Keller joined us, a Missouri-raised lover-of-land, looking for community and a place to call her own, just like the rest of us. Three other Lesbians (one couple) have built houses since then. Two of them have left, as well as my partner, Terri. In 2014, five Lesbians were living at Hawk Hill.

I was a very strong separatist on my arrival and am still, but what it means in my personal life has changed, living in a very sparsely populated area where there are more cattle than humans and where we must depend on others in ways I never imagined in the city.

We also evolved a policy of interaction almost as soon as we arrived. We loved our two widow neighbors, one now dead, and

Susan Wiseheart at Hawk Hill.

spent time at both houses in various activities, and they came here. We joined the local fire department, and some of us served on the board or were trained to fight brush fires or audited the books or were part of the auxiliary, helping raise money for equipment and operating expenses. We got to know our woman mail carrier, who lives on the next road over, and the proprietors of the nearby old country store (which the dairy refuses to supply because they don't sell enough to make it worth it).

We also joined several other organizations that put us in touch with the local (meaning a hundred-mile radius) artists and progressives, ecologists, and activists. Some of us went to peace marches. I recently attended a wedding of two straight people in their twenties.

Losing two of our residents to breakups was hard, but we figured it out as best we could. We all attended counseling together and we had mediation about another issue once.

Even harder has been losing Pat Patton in 2013. She moved to one of the nearby small towns because, approaching her mid-seventies, she was ready to be done with all that is required of living way out here in The In-Between, as one worker in an office referred to our neighborhood.

Learning about hay came early in our tenure here. We have good fields for hay that would be even better if we put money and energy into them. For years, we found people to hay them either for pay or for shares, and we spent days out there bucking bales in the heat and humidity, using it for some of the animals and for mulching our gardens.

Finding work for money was challenging, but we all managed, doing a variety of jobs both on and off the land, including nursing, massage, office work, farmwork, construction, clerking, research, census-taking, having rental properties in a nearby city, babysitting, and running a highly regarded business, eventually from home. I may even be forgetting a few.

When we came here, we all had ideas about what it would mean to live in community with each other, all responsible to take care of the land in a careful way, as the trust is set up for that purpose. Our ideas changed and evolved as we came up against various things we had to figure out or work out.

For me, moving South from Michigan and out of a city was huge. My antiracism work underwent big changes, along with everything else in my life. I am in the South. Or, um, I am in the Midwest. Depends on who is defining. Definitely, I am in a key state of the Civil War, where feelings are still very present about that not-so-long-ago war. And, in the twenty-six years I have been here, the kinds of things that need antiracist intervention have evolved and changed, too. I see more people of color in the small towns. I have learned the history. I am as good an ally as I can be, and I never do enough. The same might be said of the issues of class, sexism, ableism, and all of the others. We live on Earth here, despite being in The In-Between. We are hooked up.

I spend times in cities and I don't know what the future may hold, nor do any of us, but I am always grateful to be here, loving the land deeply and the waters and air and weather, the other dykes in my (five-or six-hour radius) neighborhood, and all of the deep intense learning I have received from a move so momentous, from city to country, from salaried professional to hourly contract worker, from a large population with plenty of cultural opportunities to a small one where the culture takes some getting used to and is often a long way off, and many other changes. It has been amazing and totally worth it.

WOMONTOWN, MISSOURI: BUILDING AN INTENTIONAL WOMYN'S URBAN COMMUNITY

B. Leaf Cronewrite and Drea Firewalker

"To walk hand in hand . . . openly."
Pamphlet for Womontown, 1989

Our desire to live in a "Womontown" sprang from a late-night discussion with each other in 1989 on our back porch in Kansas City, Missouri, as we sat listening to police sirens. "Wouldn't it be nice if our Lesbian friends lived in these apartments now occupied by bigots and bought these boarded up homes? We could walk hand in hand, openly without harassment." We began to talk about change, being able to share our daily lives in a safe and supportive place. We knew we could not restrict who wanted to live in the neighborhood of three-story shirtwaist homes interspersed with six- to eighteen-unit apartment buildings. But we would actively find Lesbians and any gay-friendly folks, preferably womyn, to help us take back our 7 × 7 block neighborhood that was historically called Longfellow/Dutch Hill.

Promotion

We created a pamphlet explaining our dreams and listing housing options and all of the Lesbian venues our city had to offer. We distributed it at potlucks and bookstores. To reach more Lesbians, we put ads in *Lesbian Connection*. The letters and phone calls from all over the United States began to pour in. About twenty-five percent of responses came from Lesbians in eight Southern states, including Missouri, looking for an out community and also affordable urban housing, jobs, college programs, and Lesbian venues in an environment with a blend of Ozark Southern culture and Midwestern "show-me" attitudes.

To Walk Hand in Hand

...Openly

Courtesy of B. Leaf Cronewrite and Drea Firewalker

WOMONTOWN

An Intentional Womyn's Urban Community in Kansas City, Missouri

Womontown pamphlet, 1989.

We met Lesbians at the airport, provided housing and meals, created social gatherings, tours of the city, and walking tours of the neighborhood with our Lesbian-friendly realtor, Ouida, who gained us access to any house for sale. We used our own money for all of our outreach and received a few donations from supportive Lesbians.

We felt an instant bond with a number of the Lesbians who came ready for a change in their lives and full of excitement to live in Womontown. Those who "got it" came back, moved in, and helped spread the word.

After visiting Womontown in 1992, Marilyn Murphy helped tell our story in her "Lesbianic Logic" column in *Lesbian News.* Several years, *Girlfriends Magazine* chose Kansas City as one of the top ten Lesbian-friendly cities, saying "Womontown is the country's only urban womyn's land."

Womontown Activities

Our sense of community was growing. On weekends, local Lesbians and Womontown Lesbians joined us at the future womyn's center, set up a grill in the yard, turned up the boom boxes, built a fence, climbed scaffolding, and painted the big house lavender. Other weekends, we were inside tearing out walls, hauling out leftover junk, putting up sheetrock—covered in dirt and paint, but smiling with arms flung around shoulders.

We organized work parties on weekends to meet U-Haul trucks and help Lesbians move in to apartments and homes. Lesbians were given the Dutch Hill tulip banner we had created to hang in their window so we all knew "where the Lesbians lived." We networked with local Lesbians to help find jobs for the Lesbians moving to Womontown who had not secured work.

Lesbians in Womontown began to gather in each other's homes for potlucks and to plan social activities. Some volunteered at Phoenix, the feminist bookstore, and at Willow Productions, the womyn's music producer. Over twenty Lesbians marched in the Pride parade behind a Womontown banner.[1]

Womontown residents in Pride march in downtown
Kansas City, 1990.

With more Lesbians in Womontown and a growing phone contact list, we all began to feel safer and more powerful. Over forty Lesbians gathered for the first "political" conversation

---

1   A picture from our neighborhood street fair is included in the book *Out in America* by Michael Goff and the staff of *Out Magazine* (New York: Viking Studio Books, 1994), 111.

about how to use the Longfellow Community Association (LCA) to take advantage of city programs like free paint or low-priced dumpsters, and grants for upgrading streetlights. We visited the elderly womyn in the neighborhood and offered them rides to the grocery or to LCA meetings. Slowly, we all began sitting openly on our porches, waving, and feeling more secure.

LCA Political Involvement

The majority of home owners and LCA members in the Longfellow/Dutch Hill neighborhood were white. The Lesbian owners and renters were about fifty percent white and fifty percent people of color.

Some in LCA felt threatened that soon they would be in the minority, based on either race or sexual preference. Some were wary that renters should have a voice or a vote in neighborhood affairs. Some thought that having too many Lesbians would bring down property values.

Some encouraged a property developer to create a Master Plan to use "eminent domain" to take property it deemed unfit. The remaining property would be brought back to the "standards," such as traditional windows and historical color selections, and uniformity of stated covenants would be enforced by fines. All standardization and "neighborhood improvements" that included addition of old-style lantern streetlamps, entrance gates with guard posts, and a brick wall periphery were to be paid for by Tax Increment Financing (TIF) funds that came from future gains from higher property taxes. Lesbians of Womontown decided to take over the association.

The LCA membership swelled from sixty to over two hundred with the addition of many Lesbians and new supporters. We created a slate of candidates who won all offices handily. Drea was President and B. Leaf (then known as Mary Ann) was Secretary and Newsletter Editor. A gay man and a Lesbian held the other offices. The LCA old-timers were shocked, and some were angry at the changes.

Our Lesbian-influenced leadership and the persistence of supporters defeated the developer's Master Plan. Lesbians' homes and the diverse neighborhood heritage were preserved. A new Master Plan without the destructive elements of the earlier plan was compiled by Karen, a Lesbian, and it was adopted. Alliances were made with other neighborhood associations to build trust. Grants for neighborhood improvement were gained. Apartment owners and some nonthreatened residents were won over. A few were not and made subtle moves to undermine the successes gained.

Womontown Success

At its peak in the early 1990s, nearly eighty Lesbians (Black, Latina, white) lived in the 7 × 7 block radius of Womontown. Most were in their twenties and thirties. Over twenty houses were sold to Lesbian families, and over forty Lesbians rented apartments. Some owners stayed awhile, rented to other Lesbians, or made periodic trips back to visit. Lesbians had a phone contact list, and every week, they fell into a rhythm of living in community, with offers of sharing skills, with a friendly wave, or just by occupying space in close proximity to other Lesbians. Some were constantly finding ways to make Womontown better. One Lesbian created a list of a hundred things that Lesbians could do to help other Lesbians in Womontown.

The two of us spent our energy constantly for three years to build the Womontown community. We realized our dream had come true. We loved having Lesbian neighbors and a safer place to live. We loved all the positive changes and wonderful Lesbians that helped create community spirit.

Womontown's Second Wave

After Lesbians settled in and got jobs, many began to expand their social circles and participate in much that Kansas City had to offer. Some made a conscious effort to create gatherings for all

Womontown Lesbians. Some chose to attend events sponsored by the local Kansas City Womyn's Support Group, Lavender Umbrella, or Lesbians of color outside Womontown. Others grew closer only to their own neighbors and friends. Some created rivalries, and vied for "leadership." As Lesbians got comfortable, they did not continue the momentum by participating as often in the community or by encouraging Lesbians they knew to move to Womontown.

As time went on, attendance fell off to Womontown potlucks or organized social events. As homes were upgraded, skill sharing lessened. Fewer Lesbians met on Saturdays for alley and vacant lot cleanup days or to attend the two-hour LCA monthly meetings to hear a police report, a grant status, or a streetlight update. Some paid little attention to the vigilance needed for midtown living.

A number of Lesbians settled in. Some chose to leave for different reasons. Others got into new relationships, then broke up, and one or both moved to another part of the city. After several years, some got homesick for family and moved back to their home state. Some chose to move to the suburbs to have a newer home or be closer to work. Some moved because as the neighborhood crime decreased and homes were improved, the home and rent prices and taxes rose, making it unaffordable for low-income Lesbians. Gay men and urban professionals moved in and made extensive renovations.

Several factors helped us decide to let our dream grow on its own. We thought we could balance our forays into the patriarchal LCA with the supportive energy of our community. Yet, struggling against the disenchanted straight LCA community drained our energy and that of our activist core of Lesbians, especially with personal threats from the angriest straight residents, who wanted to create a whole new neighborhood association. Constantly encouraging local Lesbians to support and move to Womontown was discouraging when they only came to Womontown to enjoy the social events. Also our emotions were drained by family responsibilities. Both of Leaf's parents, suffering from dementia in nearby Kansas, required a lot of her care and eventually died in 1991. Drea had to fly to Illinois to manage her grandmother's care and then her affairs after she succumbed to cancer. In 1993, Leaf's job transferred to Atlanta, so we opted for a break, keeping our property in anticipation of returning after a few years.

Vestiges of Womontown still exist twenty years later. About thirty Lesbians still live in Womontown today. Most know each other, and some spontaneous gatherings still occur in backyards and porches to talk about the height of the Womontown days. A few Lesbians and some of the new residents continue to participate in LCA.

We visit in the spring and fall, staying in our studio apartment behind our apartment building. Our main residence is in Atlanta. The last time we were visiting Kansas City, we were gratified when two young Lesbians walking down the alley stopped at our apartment yard where we were working and said, "We heard this neighborhood was called Womontown. That's why we moved here." We smiled.

"A SAGA OF LESBIAN PERSEVERANCE AND STEADFAST RESOLVE:" THE HENSONS AND CAMP SISTER SPIRIT

Marideth Sisco

"A saga of lesbian perseverance and steadfast resolve is unfolding in the South. Camp Sister Spirit is seen by many as an important symbol for increased lesbian visibility. They are proud and strong dykes and a model for all of us who are facing difficult times on the land."

—Sina Anahita, *Maize* 40 (1994): 11

I first came to Sister Spirit, just east of Hattiesburg, Mississippi, in 1995, at the end of a research trip I had taken farther south. But I had met the Hensons way earlier when they rolled into the Midwest Wimmin's Festival calling themselves "The Dixie Dykes." They had brought their little crafts booth and were fundraising, they said, to try to put together a feminist bookstore in Gulfport, Mississippi. They were an energetic, round-cheeked pair with an almost evangelical fervor for their work—to educate and bring the ideals of feminism to the women of the South.

By the time we saw them the next year, they had gotten involved with Robin Tyler, who was then promoting the Southern Women's Music and Comedy Festival in north Georgia, and who was encouraging their efforts. They had also tangled with the folks at Rhythm Fest, another Southern festival, but the Hensons explained they had different aims for a festival. The other festivals were run as businesses and out to make a profit. Sister Spirit,[1] they

---

1 Sister Spirit is the name of the nonprofit service and advocacy organization that the Hensons established in 1989. Camp Sister Spirit is the name of the 120 acres of land they bought in 1991, when Gulfport, Mississippi, would no longer host the Gulf Coast Women's Festival.

explained, aimed to become a feminist adult education center. They wanted, they said, to change women's lives. They held festivals for some years in various locations and, finally with the help of financing from some women of means in the New Orleans area, managed to buy a scrubby little run-down farm in Jones County, where the illiteracy rate among women was somewhere above thirty percent and women, white or Black, were at the bottom of the heap.

They had their share of friction among their own when Wanda, blue-collar daughter of Pentecostals, tangled with white-collar urban "lipstick" Lesbians who couldn't quite see her as being in the same pool. She was uppity, obstinate, and opinionated—and absolutely driven to bring her suffering, closeted sisters up out of the pit. With equally loving and hot-tempered agitator Brenda by her side, she couldn't be stopped.

Then one of the camp's newsletters, which credited the success of the fledgling venture to "good Lesbian energy," got into the hands of a nearby Baptist Church, and the fight was on. Gunshots in the night. Dead pets. Nails in the driveway, and Brenda's car run off the rural road. A granddaughter coming up to visit prompted a rumor that these evil Lesbians were now stealing area children. It was ugly. They put out a call for reinforcements, and women from all walks and all parts of the country came. But in many cases, the ones who responded were no more equipped for life under siege than those already there. Wanda, who was on disability after a fall at work had injured her back and hip, had to have a stern talk with her son, Arthur, telling him, "If they come for us you'll have to help me, because I can't run." When I heard of the situation, I begged them to pull out, to come up to Missouri and lay low until things settled down. It wasn't Wanda's style. Instead, she called Oprah and dared the other side to meet her there. They did. That, too, was ugly. The best line of the day was when the Baptist minister tried to explain to Oprah that she just didn't understand the ways of Mississippians. "I was born in Mississippi," Oprah returned in a cold voice. "I understand it just fine."[2]

(l to r) Brenda Henson, Wanda Henson, and Marideth Sisco, 1995, in front of the Camp Sister Spirit main building that was meeting room, archives, kitchen, and pantry downstairs, with a bunkhouse up top.

But time went on, and just what the Baptists feared happened. Over time, people got to know them, and realized they were just people. And the perception in the community of Camp Sister Spirit began to change. But by then Wanda was exhausted and in debt, and Brenda had cancer. They stepped aside and let others carry

---

2 The Hensons were on the Oprah show in December 1993. In 1994, they were on *20/20*, *The Jerry Springer Show*, and *Larry King Live,* as reported in *Out in the South*, ed. Carlos L. Dews and Carolyn Leste Law (Philadelphia: Temple University Press, 2001), p. 65. See also Bill Turque and Kevin Gray. "Mississippi Burning." *Newsweek* 122.25 (December 20, 1993): 33–35. Bonnie J. Morris covers the troubles at Camp Sister Spirit and quotes Wanda Henson at length in Chapter 8 of *Eden Built by Eves: The Culture of Women's Music Festivals* (New York: Alyson Books, 1999), 222–53.

on. And those others passed it to others, with each generation of leadership less able, and those gone before still trying to heal. There's no question they made their place in Ovett, Mississippi. The proof of that came when Hurricane Katrina hit the poverty-stricken community. Women, mostly Lesbians from all across the country who had visited there in earlier times, loaded their trucks with chainsaws, nonperishable foods, and dollars and came to help. A few days later, a note appeared on the door of the local firehouse. "We've been up too many nights, and we've got to get some sleep. If you need anything, go on down to the camp. The girls will take care of you." Folks at the general store now refer to that original outraged Baptist as "that little Hitler." They're over it.

But the land is now idle, the buildings empty. Brenda passed in 2008. Wanda opened her little medical clinic down on the coast and treats victims of the Deepwater Horizon spill. It might be considered a failure, overall. Except everyone who set foot on that little patch of earth in the Mississippi pine belt was changed by it, challenged to show their best, and worst, and depths of character and courage they would not have imagined themselves to possess. I don't think any of them saw themselves as having engaged in any vital part of the history of civil rights. But the women of color over in Hattiesburg, I'll wager, would beg to differ. We saw it in their eyes in the checkout line in the grocery stores, where we got accustomed to people who had read the local paper and its stories of "that business over in Ovett." We expected they would move away from us and steer their children clear so nothing of our difference would rub off. The clerks, on the other hand, would break into wide smiles and whisper softly and so their mouths moved hardly at all, and say "Come on, girl, come on up, honey, we're with you." What we took away from that experience humbled us. We are none of us the same. It is too soon to know whether that small encampment in the Pine Belt will just fade quietly into the history of Jones County or will become known as the "Stonewall of the South." What we know is that we who were there were changed fundamentally.

ALAPINE: MORGANA'S MAGICAL MOUNTAIN: (1997—PRESENT)

Rose Norman

In the mid-1990s, three Pagoda residents decided to sell their Vilano Beach (Florida) cottages and start over in the mountains of rural northern Alabama. It marked a shift from an urban beach resort community to a rural Southern environment. It was also an end to an impressive herstory of art exhibits, dance, theater, women's music, and other events that Pagoda sponsored at the Center (see "The Pagoda, Temple of Love," p. 53). Morgana MacVicar, her partner Fayann Schmidt, and friend Barbara Lieu formed a corporation and bought 275 acres in northeast Alabama. Of that, 108 acres were divided into two-acre lots that they sold to Lesbians, starting in 1997.

A 2009 *New York Times* article describes the community twelve years after that move.[1] In more recent interviews,[2] cofounder Morgana MacVicar describes her original vision for Alapine. Barbara Lieu, another longtime Pagoda resident, explains why they left Pagoda and what happened when they got to Alapine. Other Alapine residents contributed their thoughts via email.

Morgana MacVicar: There's a magic to this mountain. That's why my aunts came here originally. It's full of fairies. In the early

---

1 Sarah Kershaw, "My Sister's Keeper," *The New York Times*, January 30, 2009, Fashion & Style section, http://www.nytimes.com/2009/02/01/fashion/01womyn.html. See also Nancy C. Unger, "From Jook Joints to Sisterspace: The Role of Nature in Lesbian Alternative Environments in the United States," in *Queer Ecologies: Sex, Nature, Politics, Desire*, ed. Catriona Mortimer-Sandilands and Bruce Erickson (Bloomington: Indiana University Press, 2010), 192–95.

2 Rose Norman interviewed Morgana MacVicar, Barbara Lieu, and four other Pagoda women at Alapine on April 13, 2013, and interviewed Barbara Lieu again on August 29, 2014. She compiled this essay from those interviews, plus emails from other Alapine women in October 2014. Rand Hall contributed to and also edited it for publication.

1930s, my aunt Alice bought a Victorian lodge that had been built when [the area] was a resort for rich people who came by railroad. She had looked all over for a mountain to start a summer camp for girls, and she said this was the one because it had the fairies. She ran that camp for thirty-seven years, Alpine [not "Alapine"] Lodge Camp for Girls. Growing up, I got to go for free—women's space for three full months for free! When Aunt Alice had a heart attack, it was sold. It became a boy's camp, and that just broke my heart. Always I yearned to be here. This was my spiritual home.

Some Alapine residents in 2010, l to r: Winnie Adams, Ann Marevis (deceased), Ellen Spangler, Jade DeForest, Barbara Moore, Jean Adele, Sonia Johnson, unidentified guest, Mary Alice Stout, Rand Hall, DeJoly LaBrier, Emily Greene.

A Lesbian friend who went to camp with me was now a realtor. She showed us the land that was already called Alapine Village.[3] When we came here, we all felt that this was right, but it required a lot of magic, meditation, and lawyers to get a clear title to it.

Barbara Lieu: At the Pagoda, we lived in a very small amount of space, eight cottages to begin with, and then another four cottages, and two two-story houses. We realized we wanted more

3 The name "Alapine," which was on the developer's map for the subdivided land, stands for Alabama Pines.

space. We also ran a business together, the Center building [at the Pagoda]. Women donated money monthly and could come and stay, or they could rent a room and vacation there. After about twenty years living at Pagoda, we realized that we didn't want to meet and make decisions any more, but just form a Lesbian neighborhood, where you would know that your neighbors were Lesbians. You wouldn't have to worry about going away on vacation and coming back to find out that the group had met and made a rule that you couldn't do something or have something on your lot. Three of us formed a corporation called Sheeba Mountain Properties, Inc. The corporation bought this land, which had already been divided up into forty-five buildable two-acre lots. With the help of an attorney, we put together a set of covenants and restrictions that you would know before you bought a lot or lots. They are filed in the county courthouse and referenced in the deed. In order to keep it as a Lesbian neighborhood, we had the deed say that Sheeba would have the right of first refusal any time anybody wanted to sell their lot. That way no one would have to meet, and there would be no business run together. We sold some of the lots, and currently, thirteen women live here full-time or part-time.

Some of the women living here wanted to do projects together and especially wanted to have a place to gather and socialize. They formed Alapine Community Association (ACA), which some residents joined. It is independent of Sheeba Mountain Properties, which continues to market the lots here that are for sale.

Pat Nolan: What I treasure about living at Alapine, as a single woman, is the ability to live way out in the woods, close to nature on a magical mountain because we have the security of being surrounded by Lesbian neighbors.

Winnie Adams: Here is something I love about rural living. This week, my neighbors flagged me down to tell me I had a flat tire. Very shortly, a man stopped to change it for me. He had to figure out how to access the tire, which turns out to be under the car, pull out the spare, and take it down the road to inflate it, change the tire, and follow me to the tire place for repair. Then he invited me to his church!

Emily Greene: After living for eleven years in Alapine, in November 2013, I moved to Greenfield, Massachusetts, to be closer to my blood family. Although there were struggles during those years at Alapine, I found it to be a great experience in learning to live in community and searching for the core of my soul. The ACA group, which I was involved with, was committed to living intentionally, sustainably, and working on helping each other "Age in Place." As anyone who has lived in community knows, it takes commitment and perseverance. I treasured the work ACA did and does to maintain a community center, communal veggie garden, and a wide array of social activities, while remaining open to outside visitors. I do miss each of them dearly.

Rand Hall: I have owned land here at Alapine since 1997 and been a full-time resident since 2007. At this point [October 2014], Alapine is a thriving community. ACA maintains and manages a community center, hosts classes, games nights, potlucks, entertainment, and fundraisers to continue to improve the accessibility of the Center. Lesbian visitors from all over the country stay at the Center to experience and participate in "Lesbian community." Most events are open to all women, though some are Lesbian-only. Participation in the Association and the events is strictly voluntary. ACA does not make any rules or have mandatory meetings. Alapine succeeds as a caring neighborhood, not a communal living situation.

For information about buying a two-acre lot at Alapine, go to alapine.wordpress.com or email alapinesales@gmail.com.

"A GREAT BIG WOMEN OF COLOR TENT:" BLANCHE JACKSON AND MAAT DOMPIM

Merril Mushroom

> "Maat is the name of the ancient African Goddess who represents balance, truth, and justice; Dompim means a place in the bush where the voice of the Goddess is heard."
>
> —*Maize* 45 (Summer 1995): 7

B lanche Jackson is a Landyke of great brilliance, eccentricity, and perseverance. Born in Brooklyn, New York, she has lived in several places and had a wide variety of life experiences. In spite of hardships, she maintains a positive perspective. Among her many talents, she is a wonderful storyteller.

I met Blanche at Sivananda Yoga Ashram in Val Morin, Québec, in 1966. I was in my shower singing "Sleeping Bee" when someone joined in from the other side of the bathroom wall. "Who the hell else knows *that* song?" I wondered. That was Blanche, and the beginning of a friendship where we have bounced in and out of each other's lives many times. (Maintaining contact with traveling women was much more difficult in the "old days" before digital technology, when we depended on the US Postal Service's deliveries and pay telephones.)

She has worked as a file clerk, senior clerk, supervising clerk, administrative assistant, UPS driver, bank messenger, office assistant, warehouse laborer, MR house counselor, halfway house "gatekeeper," library aide, yoga teacher, gardener, small trucker, craftswoman, thrift shop manager, census worker, school bus aide, and companion. She has done lectures and workshops, run a cultural crafts and merchandising business, and distributed a line of Mountain Mama spices.

In the early 1970s, Blanche moved from her New York City apartment into a loft. "I needed a loft to train myself for country living,"[1] she says. She planted a garden on the roof and fertilized it with horse manure that she hauled from the police stable nearby. She had bought an old bread truck that she named Mariposa, and started Wonder Wimmin Trucking. She hauled vegetables for the People's Warehouse (a collection of neighborhood co-ops), the Integral Yoga Health Food Store, etc.

In an unpublished memoir, Blanche tells this story of going to a women's concert in 1976:

> After it was over, there was a request for someone with a truck to help return rented equipment. I charged rudely to the stage for fear someone would beat me to it. (Yeah right.) Soon I was a working member of Lesbian Feminist Liberation. LFL published "The Feminist," produced dances, concerts (including the one I had attended), and discussion events, all of which were massively attended, but usually about six of us showed up for work meetings. If I remember correctly there was one Native American womyn and two of us identified as Black.

In the late 1970s, Blanche and a girlfriend showed up out of nowhere at my remote Tennessee hill farm. She had taken a notion to come visit me from New York City. With no GPS to tell her where I lived, she arrived in the nearby town, went to the local post office, and asked for directions to my house, which she was given.

In the early 1980s, Blanche went to a Quaker Lesbian conference at Heathcote community in Maryland. Heathcote was looking for new members, and Blanche and her partner Amoja, wanting to garden on the earth whereof they walked instead of the roof where they lived, moved there. They had a garden and grew gourds that they crafted into shakerees (percussion instruments) with fishing line and beads. They sold the first half-

---

1 Quoted from an unpublished memoir written for this issue. Much of the background reported here, before Maat Dompim, is paraphrased from that memoir.

dozen immediately at a music festival, and thus was born Market Wimmin, their cultural crafts and merchandising business, which also published Amoja's book *Cultural Etiquette: A Guide for the Well-Intended* (1990).

They began to travel the festival circuit, selling their merchandise and doing workshops and seminars. Here Blanche picks up the story.[2]

> We were going to Michigan [Womyn's Music Festival] and North East Women's Music Retreat (NEWMR) every year. . . . Women of color who worked at both of those festivals would have a meeting under a tree at NEWMR every year to go over their experiences. The first year I went, the topic came up that, you know, you see a sister on the path, and then you never see her again, because there's 3000 people there. First we thought of having a women of color campground, but that seemed too much like segregated housing. So somebody said, what about a resource tent for women of color who want to connect or who want to share cultural stuff? We'd have reading materials and all that. So everybody agreed that's what we wanted, a resource tent.
>
> . . . .
>
> Amoja and some other women contacted both festivals about this resource tent. NEWMR said yes right away. Michigan thought it would be divisive—we should all be sisters together, melded and everything. . . . I kept both festivals up to date on my efforts to transport lower income wimmin, which resulted in five vans to NEWMR and three to Michigan. At Michigan, the vans were incorporated into the shuttle system. Amoja and some other people went and negotiated really hard at Michigan . . ., and they got half of a tent, I think the political tent. It overflowed. Women flocked to it. Michigan the next year gave us a small tent, and they

---

2   This and all subsequent quotations are from a recorded telephone interview that Rose Norman did with Blanche Jackson on July 20, 2014.

overflowed that, and so the tents grew bigger. Those tents are where the discussions took place about what women of color want. If there was women of color land, what would they want?

. . . .

We had been doing workshops at women's festivals about women's land and what women would want in a land site. The way I thought about it personally was not so much that it was women of color land, as that it was land that reflected the cultures and values of women of color. Personally, I didn't care who came, but I wanted the culture and the atmosphere to be reflective of many cultures. Not only Black—I meant diasporic African, African-American, Native American, Latina, Asian. I wanted to do something that offered something to all of those groups.

Amoja Three Rivers at Womonwrites, 1990s.

If we're going to have women of color land, we don't want it to be twenty women sitting around negotiating who's going to do the laundry or cook dinner that night. I wanted a place where individual women, where as many women as possible could use it. We needed a system, and a structure, and a game plan that would accommodate a *flow of women* rather than a static community. This was hard to convey. People kept asking me about the community I was trying to start, and I kept saying, "I'm not trying to start a community. I want to develop a facility."

Another thing we wanted was some place that was not busy, busy, busy. The festivals were a great place to meet people, but they weren't a great place to explore relationships or develop anything permanent. Everybody's running to workshops and to this place and that place. We wanted a place for communication and contemplation.

During one of their festival circuit trips, the cabin where Blanche and Amoja had been living when they were not on the road burned to the ground with all their possessions—books, clothing, craft supplies, everything. Women donated toward their recovery so generously that, as Blanche said, "We went right from disaster relief into fundraising for this land."

During the land search, they stayed for a while at WIT's End farm in Tennessee (see p. 106), house sitting. Then, while renting a house in Auto, West Virginia, from a gay boy who had built the house himself, they found the land they were looking for in Buckingham County, Virginia. In order to be closer to the new land, they moved into a place that was slightly renovated from an old juke joint. (The history of the juke joint is a story in itself.)

In the beginning of their work on Maat Dompim, Blanche says,

Women were enthusiastic. They'd say, "If you get a place, I'm in!" A woman who had written about her experience on some women of color land in another state said, "If it's in Virginia it would be more convenient for me, but wherever you do it, I'm there!" People would say, "When you get the nonprofit status, we will come." (We did that in 1992.) Then they said, "When you get the land, we will come." And we did (1998), and they did, and they oohed and ahhed, volunteered to do things, and then went home and failed to follow through.

Blanche Jackson at Womonwrites in Fall 2011.

Then Amoja got sick and had surgery. Right after she came home from the hospital, they were evicted from the juke joint, because the landlady's family members wanted to use it. Blanche had her hands full with caregiving and trying to make enough income to live on. She had thirty days to find another home and move all their belongings. One day, she came home to find Amoja gone and a note on the table. Amoja had gone back to her family in Minnesota. Blanche put their things in storage and rented an old trailer from a fellow she refers to as the "scumlord." She said it was like living in a cracked can:

> All that threw me into ongoing permanent survival mode. I've been trying to figure out what to do with the land ever since. I tried to give it away. One of the problems is that the access road needs work. The land itself is beautiful. It has some of the most beautiful views. It's 109 acres, and then there's another 24 acres under a quit claim deed.

"I've tried to find other groups who would take it over," Blanche says. The land is paid for, but back taxes are owed that she has been unable to squeeze out the money for. Although the nonprofit has lapsed (but could be reinstated), the not-for-profit (Maat Dompim) still exists and owns the land. Nobody is living there. Every so often, someone shows up who seems interested, and then they go back home again, and that's the end of it. Blanche says,

> I thought the women of color land would be like a great big women of color tent. We tried to write the core proposal for the land project like a honeycomb, so that it had a firm structure, but a lot of open spaces where women could plug anything in. . . .
>
> You know, it's funny. There'll be all these positive omens and signs, and suddenly everything comes together! And then everything falls apart.

WHY I'M NOT ON WOMEN'S LAND[1]

Juana Maria Paz

This piece was originally published in Maize *in 1984, when the author was in her early thirties. Since writing it, she spent seven years at Twin Oaks, a mixed gender, primarily heterosexual, intentional community in Virginia. Today, she lives with her daughter and grandson in Richmond, Virginia. Additions to the original piece are indicated by italics.*

After reading the second issue of *Maize*, I am struck with the fact that most women's lands are sparsely populated. I learned recently that Cabbage Lane in Oregon is empty even though it's paid for and has cabins. OWL Farm is in jeopardy, and a woman recently said to me, "Why don't women live there?" To which I replied, "Are you going back?"

"No," she said, "I can't make a living there, but women with money could do it. With all those women on the west coast, I don't know why they can't find women who want to live there."

"I know why," I said, "because it's too insecure. The land and cabins might be secure, but that's all. Anyone who can afford to live somewhere else doesn't want to take the risk, and the people who are insecure financially are not in a good position to try it."

I think women's lands have remained on the fringes of the women's movement because mystery, controversy, and secrecy surround them. I wonder how many groups exist that don't want publicity and why not. I wonder how many connections have been made between city and country women through *Lesbian Connection's* Land Directory. *Publicity was a double-edged sword. How could we do outreach for support and not advertise our*

---

[1] Originally published in *Maize* 3 (1984): 8–10, when the author was living in Fayetteville, Arkansas.

location to the general public? I think this was a weakness of the communication system at the time, which was mostly print and paper through the mail.

Many urban women dismiss country living as separatist escapism and white flight, and many don't seem to know that there are women of color lands, also. Hopefully, the upcoming *Lesbians on Land* anthology will fill this information gap.[2] Women's land has no organized lobbies like ERA and abortion have. There seems to be a veil of secrecy around past and present lands, presumably because of conflict, legal battles, and differences of opinion. If land groups continue to form, struggle, and disband in turmoil and silence, I doubt if they will ever be taken seriously.

I think women have got to start talking, and we have to admit failure. Americans equate failure with dishonor and will do almost anything to avoid or deny it, but all the problems could be a temporary setback if we would evaluate them to determine the necessary conditions for success.

Groups that have split up on bad terms are unlikely to issue joint statements, and while the ethics of sharing partial and individual accounts are being explored, I think something has to happen besides silence and the horror stories and rumors that circulate regularly. *I am sure some women wanted zero publicity. I always thought it was better to be clear about the pros and cons and where we were at on the land—self-sufficient or struggling, mostly getting along or high turnover—as this gave potential to women considering joining us.*

I should introduce myself, at this point, as the author of a book on Lesbian of color land, *The La Luz Journal*, who spent 1978 and

---

2 Joyce Cheney's *Lesbian Land* came out the following year (Minneapolis: Word Weavers, 1985) and includes Juana Maria Paz's "La Luz de la Lucha: Excerpts from *The La Luz Journal*," about women of color land in California (pp. 66–72) and "Where Do Dreams Go When They Die?" (pp. 72–75). Other articles by Juana Maria Paz include "Intentional Community Building at Twin Oaks," *off our backs* (April 1991): 22–24; "Communal Living, Feminist Education and Group Process," *off our backs* (November 1992): 17, 19; "Women on the Land: Lesbian Land and Community Building," *off our backs* (June 1994):12–13; "Community-Building Workshops," *The Womyn on the Land Network* 15 (November 1995): 1–2.

1979 traveling between different women's lands in the United States. I have lived at La Luz in California, OWL Farm in Oregon, visited ARF in New Mexico, Cabbage Lane and Rainbow's End in Oregon, and spent time at Rainbow Land [Arco Iris] and Sassafras in Arkansas. I consider myself a strong proponent of women's land and feel I have seen the best and worst of what it has to offer. These are my views on the obstacles they face or, more personally, the reasons why I do not go back.

First of all, I don't think anyone already on women's land wants to live with me. If this seems like too personal a reason, imagine living in the middle of nowhere with people who don't want you there. If there were people who wanted the pleasure of my company, I would need to know on what terms and have that spelled out in advance. Since people often don't know what we want and have to offer, the process can break down right here, and I would not even visit without clear expectations. As far as why I don't feel others want to live with me, it's more a lack of real conviction that I feel than anything else. I don't think anyone can say to me, "Juana, I want to live with you because . . ., etc." in a very active and specific sense. I hear all this generalization about "Gee, we really need support," and "I wish more women would come," without a realization that it is not going to just "happen." It needs to be worked out. My own reason for not wanting to live with women is not knowing what I can count on them for, or what I should realistically expect and have no way to figure out without a willingness on women's parts, collectively, to deal with these tender issues.

I can't go further without stating my motivations. I came from a violent, abusive family in a northern city, so I probably had mega-illusions about rural life. I had grown up reading the Daily News, *so for me Lesbian land offered the possibility of a life without violence and unfairness. But it was not just an absence of those things that I craved. It was what I wanted to put in their place. I always hoped if I stayed long enough, there would be an independent feminist school. I wanted art, creativity, children, planting, and a plethora of projects to be thriving in the spaces we made, and I'm not saying none of that happened. I had not anticipated that the "more oppressed than thou" would get so out of hand. There was support, friendship, good times, and real accomplishment. But for me it was overshadowed by the oneups"woman"ship. I don't think this was deliberate or malicious. We rewarded people for confronting oppression, and all of a sudden if you had a music tape with one male artist, we had a problem, and talking could go on and on . . . None of us would have wanted to shut women up, but when we each became the oppressor for somebody else, we didn't know what to do.*

Where would I live? Most women's lands have very few structures, and I doubt if owners are prepared to build cabins for future residents. It would be foolish of me to build on a place where I have no legal rights and no assurance that I will be able to stay long enough to enjoy it.

Aside from material and economic factors—food, money, transportation, shelter, firewood, raising animals, etc.—the decision to stay or leave is often based on relationships. Can we get along with the other people there? If so, is the support of a handful of people, with varying levels of involvement in our lives and struggles, really enough? Pressure from the need to get along can alienate people who do not want such loaded relationships anyway. *The process to deal with this was endless meetings. I am not sure we put time limits on those. There may have been an unquestioned assumption that every person having their say would lead to community. I do think there was a lot of posturing about this, and using language and communication as sport, maybe not words as weapons exactly, not all the time, but definitely talking for effect.*

People generally resist the sense of duty, obligation, and interdependence that characterizes true community involvement. That is, we *say* we want a women's community, but we are always letting each other know that we do not want to be bothered, we do not like to feel obligated. We treat each other like outsiders and without respect, and we do not want to take other people's needs into consideration. This excludes most groups and individuals from my definition of community.

When we talk about living in community, we usually mean getting our own needs met, and we concentrate on how nice that would be, for a change. But when we don't consider what we will have to do in return, and accept all the burdens and obligations involved, we lose sight of the fact that every single person has to do her part in order for there to be a community in the first place.

The lesson seems to be that necessary conditions for success include each member having a major investment in the group's survival, as well as allegiance to the entire community, not just their own mate, lover, or family. Also, just about everyone who has ever lived communally complains about the lack of privacy.

In some ways, we were all unrealistic in what we expected from women's land, but we were also led to believe that if we "gave our all" to women, we would be rewarded. We were urged on by individual and collective visions of feminist utopia. We need to watch that because every time we exaggerate what we can actually do for women in order to get support, we increase the level of mistrust and disappointment a little more. *The differences between a women's fantasy of what life would be like on the land, and the reality and rewards of living on the land are probably very personal and a rich area of exploration. It might have made a better meeting topic than do we want dogs in the main house, and how many? all the time? etc.*

When I visited Blue Lunden at Sugarloaf Key, she said something that stayed with me: "This is more than I bargained for. . . . I didn't sign up for this . . ." Generally, she observed that things took longer and were harder than she originally expected or anticipated. I said to myself then, and many times since, "Well, isn't that a truism of human endeavor?" We each probably surprise ourselves at our levels and depths of strength, despair, over-explaining, etc.

No matter what we want or are led to believe, we need to realize that there is a price to be paid for living in community—in terms of individual freedom and self-determination. Sometimes the survival of the group will conflict with our own needs. Are we prepared for this? We say we want a women's community, but do we know what it will take—from each person—to make that happen? If so, are we prepared to do what needs to be done, at the time it needs to happen, or only when we feel like it?

I remember writing in my journal years ago that as long as the land existed, there was hope for the future, but I no longer believe that availability of land is the major obstacle. The point is—do we want to live on land in groups? Can we support each other and sustain a community? What about when it is hard, when we do not feel like it, when we "need space," etc.? Do we want to make commitments and sacrifices, work at it for years and really deal with each other—enough to make it happen? Are we in it for the long haul, or are we only available for the good times?

No amount of words, rhetoric, and matriarchal descriptions will turn a piece of land (or any other location) into a thriving women's community. Only we can do that, and it will take soul-searching analysis and an enormous amount of effort and energy from everyone involved. *[Women's land communities] were a noble effort, and one of the things I gave up by leaving [women's land] was the belief that I was participating in something that promised great changes and great hope for the planet.*

I am sure that people will want to know if I went straight. I have been celibate about sixty of my almost sixty-two years, and have had very few intimate partners, a few male and a few female. For me, the lure of women's land was the blank canvas that we could fill with our own culture and interests, so when that mostly did not happen, I just left. But I would not want anyone to take my experience as proof you should never do that, or that living collectives are not manageable. What I would like for all of us is discernment on how to proceed while trying hard things and creating new forms. Just because something is not easy doesn't mean it is not worthwhile.

FAMILY TREE

Loba Wakinyan

Driving across Whiteside Mountain[1]
Named after our runaway ancestors
We took a sharp left

My great-aunt and her unnamed wife met us at the door
Of a tiny one-room cabin
The woodstove nearly baking the marrow in our bones
As we stepped through

The back wall was lined with mason jars
Of vegetables, fruits, pickles, jellies, and jams
The other three walls were bookshelves
Packed to the ceiling
Where herbs and plants hung down

Their daughter and her girlfriend—
My cousins—
Came in behind us

I couldn't stop grinning
I'd found my people
Within my people

Upon a great white mountain
Full of slow hillbilly drawl
Related and stranger at once

My cousins kept smiling back at me
And giving each other that knowing look

---

1 Whiteside Mountain is near Highlands, North Carolina.

Before inviting me to help them gather
Apples from the orchard outside

We laughed and picked and laughed
As they comfortably touched and kissed each other
More women came into the trees

My face flushed with excitement
Relieved from my own adolescent shame

We returned to their mothers' cabin
With our pick
Then they took me to their own
Tiny tin shed cabin,
With a rainbow hanging just outside the door,
Tucked between a dozen other small Lesbian shacks

I smiled and said "nice flag"
Together we laughed
And I knew
I had just come home

WHERE ARE THE YOUNG ONES TO TAKE OUR PLACE?: INTERVIEWS WITH YOUNG WOMEN LIVING IN MIDDLE TENNESSEE[1]

Merril Mushroom

*W**here are the young ones to take our place?* This question often has been on the minds and tongues of many of us old dykes. Who will take over the land/politics/activism/etc./etc./etc., after we die? We may or may not have children/grandchildren who may or may not follow in our footsteps. In any event, we wonder who will continue with the Lesbian-feminist tradition that was so important to us in the latter decades of the last century, and who will preserve and nurture our land, our world?

One of the places the young ones are is here in rural Middle Tennessee. We are blessed to have a huge and thriving GLBTQ community made up of overlapping circles of collectives, households, couples, and individuals of many non-heteronormative (hereafter referred to as NHN) persuasions. Gender identity tends to be fluid among many of the NHN folks, but others identify definitively as radical fairies (men and women both), Lesbian, transgender, or queer. The communities are fairly intergenerational with ages ranging mostly from twenties to fifties. Many of them arrived in their twenties and thirties and have been here ten or fifteen years. Several of us are in our seventh decade or older. There are very few children. There is a wide range of socioeconomic and cultural backgrounds, but the population is largely Caucasian with a painful awareness of this fact and plenty of white guilt and desire for and movement toward change. The

---

1 In August and September 2014, Merril Mushroom interviewed six women, aged thirty to forty, living in rural Middle Tennessee: Matilda (b. 1984), Swamprat (b. 1983), Lauren (b. 1980), Emily (b. 1979), Beef (b. 1976), and Krista (b. 1973).

queer intentional community called IDA has set up a safe space for queer people of color, and the residents do anti-oppression workshops.

Ten years ago, two young women I barely knew who lived at IDA knocked on my door, marched into my living room, sat themselves down on the sofa, and announced, "We're feminists!" Somehow, they knew I would like hearing that, and I did! Many of the NHN folks do identify as feminist and are very active around issues to do with racism, homophobia, prison and immigration issues, environmental concerns, mental health, etc. However, I find much less activism around issues of sexism, and most of what there is comes from the women. Many of the men – gay though they might be – talk a better line than they actually walk, and many of the women have commented about the misogyny they experience in the community.

Over the past twelve years or so, I have had numerous conversations with the young NHN women out here and have begun recording interviews with them for the Southern Lesbian Feminist Activist Herstory Project. Most of them have lived here for at least several years. Some have lived collectively before they came here, some live on the collectives now, and some live by themselves, as couples, or in small households. They all are womyn born and womyn still; some identify as Lesbian, most identify as queer, and some don't want a static label. But all of them strongly identify as feminist and feel that feminist values and practices are the right way to live in the world. They are pro-peace, pro-environment, pro-tolerance, pro-community, and they work toward putting this into practice in their daily lives.

When Swamprat identifies as a feminist, she explains it this way:

It means I think everybody, regardless of their journey, deserves to be on equal footing as far as power and access and rights and privileges. . . . I think feminism is fundamentally anti-oppressive, so it extends into other forms of anti-oppressions, such as oppression against people who are not white, or against the earth, or against native peoples or poor people. When I think of feminism, I think of being against patriarchy, which doesn't just oppress women but also the earth, poor people, and people of color. . . . Lesbian-feminism is, like, our roots, what brought us to where we are. It gives us certain freedoms, political freedoms obviously, but also social freedoms and a breadth of ideas that have evolved through the years of feminism, the waves of feminism.[2]

I see all these young women as Landykes, whether they live individually, collectively, or something in between, even though many of these young women were not aware of the Lesbian land movement, *Shewolf's Directory*, *Maize*, or other Landyke publications. Many do know about *Lesbian Connection*, and some have attended Womonwrites or MichFest. They all are committed to living on the land. They live simply and rough, use chainsaws, weedeaters, and other hand and power tools of the country. They drive tractors and know about firearms. They cut firewood, garden, raise animals, and try to live in harmony with nature. They are active to varying degrees in anti-oppression work, and they participate to varying degrees with the locals and the greater rural community.

The pitfalls of collective living don't seem to have changed much since the 1970s, nor have the approaches to trying to bridge these pits. Some of the groups want to be open to everyone as a sanctuary, with no rules, everyone accepted and supported. This does not always play out well in real life. The collectives still have many and lengthy meetings and endless processing and decisions made that then may not be followed through on. Sometimes people do have to be asked to leave. There may be arduous and painful dramas, inconsideration on the parts of visitors who come

---

2 From the interview with Swamprat (Erica Fullbright) at Merril's home near Dowelltown, Tennessee, on September 10, 2014.

and feel free to act out however they please and then go away, while the residents still have to live there. Some of the issues cited in the interviews were passive-aggressive behavior, and inability to recognize and deal with problems early on, to nip them in the bud before they get out of hand. Other issues include lack of structure and boundaries, lack of agreed-upon guidelines, people's egos, interpersonal dynamics and gossip, and negativity.

When asked what might help, Swamprat replied:

People just got to get right with themselves, I guess. Being responsible, self-aware, being willing to be called out. Feeling good enough about themselves that they . . . can actually hear when other people have grievances about their behavior, actually hear it and not take it on, just work on it . . . work on personal growth and awareness.

THE ACHE
Rachel

t is 2009. The West Virginia intentional community was founded years ago in support of a guru. Today, a handful of caretakers continue to enact ceremonies and read the literature of this inspirational person. Lofty, magnificent buildings are empty most of the year. I am a rootless traveler. I have finished a job, gotten on a Greyhound, and arrived here for the contact improv jam. The weekend is part improvised dancing, part temporary intentional community hosted within the landed community.

If contact improv has not crossed your path, it is an egalitarian dance form. Physically smaller people learn to use gravity and motion to their advantage, and are able to lift larger people on their bodies, on their backs, in the air, etc. The dance can be as simple as lying on the floor, feeling microsensations. It can involve rolling on the floor, jumping up, flying through the air, landing on another rolling person, being lifted on a back, or torso, side, or leg, then doing the lifting.

At this weekend event, I feel an ache. For one, I have not yet moved to the intentional community where I will meet my future wife. But even without a woman to love, I ache for women-only space. This is before my five- to seven-year journey of discovering what I like to call Lesbian separatism within myself. I feel a burning itch of annoyance that my body is physically touching men so repeatedly during the contact improv jam.

The event creates a community for three days. We sit in a circle to generate the weekend schedule. Meetings are supposed to be egalitarian, like the dance form, and have decentralized leadership. The youngest in the group (and shy at that time), I bring my suggestion to the meeting. "During this weekend, I would love to have a women-only jam." The group of thirty or so people discusses pros and cons of the idea, mostly cons. As fifty percent of the people are men, their voices factor significantly in the debate. It shifts from being about a women-only dance time—a time not to have men's bodies rubbing up against our bodies, my body—to a different concept. Now the idea is a dance performance piece to play with or reflect on gender. It will still involve fifty percent of dance partners being male, but through narrative or spoken word the theatrical dance will talk about gender.

How would this resolve my dilemma of not wanting men to touch my body with their bodies? The issue is not considered. A brief but lively debate ensues about "the gender dance." Ultimately, the idea is dropped.

I stay after the event as a two-weeklong volunteer. The one other traveler/volunteer (I'll call him James) cannot fathom why I'm not sexually interested in him. He diagnoses me as asexual. Meanwhile, I have passionate conversations with a member of the community (I'm going to call her Marjorie) about us being attracted to each other. She tugs my heartstrings until the end of an afternoon together painting her bathroom. We put away the paint supplies and sit down. Marjorie tells me she is fully heterosexual and does not like me that way anymore. Plus she had a dream about this man she is definitely going to date, and their relationship will be exactly one year, she can feel it.

With patches I have sewn on my corduroys, with a backpack, I move on from West Virginia. I am gradually coming out as Lesbian. I do not think about this phrase "Lesbian separatist" yet, but every women's space that I encounter amazes and delights me. Two or three summers of the local women's campout, the women's college that I go to and I admire. I had attended the contact improv jam during time off from college, which is my women's college mother ship. A stranded intergalactic traveler, I had asked for permission from contact improv men to hold a women-only dance. After the idea morphed and then got shut down, my women's ache and Lesbian ache both internally intensify.

Must return to women's college.

Must return to women's college.

I do believe that feminist men exist, and that all men should strive to become feminists. Likewise, all humans should strive to fight inequalities of racism, ableism, free trade capitalism, and so many social diseases. But I no longer believe that debating with feminist or nonfeminist men about the value of women-only space is a replacement for actually being in women's space.

I often hear from older Lesbian-feminist friends that younger women are not showing up to join womyn's lands. I want to come forward and say I exist, both to the feminist elders that I admire, and to mainstream society. I exist as a young woman who is Lesbian, not "queer." Women's lands have the potential to see new energy and new membership.

There are different parts to my activist self. Sometimes I worry that taking care of my own healing is privileged. A part of me believes I should only focus on wars, refugees, the prison system, homelessness, and the deepest social ills. Yes, those things are priorities. But . . . that part of me can be capable of memory loss. Have I already forgotten that in 2010 the Mormon church pushed to defeat California's marriage equality? It is not a given that I will be accepted or safe in this world, in every time and place.

The young generation can believe that Lesbian-feminist goals have been fully reached. With lack of historical/herstorical memory, it is no wonder that young women do not come to womyn's lands. From my personal experience, my real-life experience, I once had an "ache." This ache was so many things to me. I felt lonely without having yet discovered a really wonderful romantic relationship. I felt alone in my desire for women-only spaces. In terms of actualizing my sexual orientation, women's spaces were a huge help. By stepping away from the numerous male friends who pressured me to be bisexual or fluid, I could finally be honest with myself. It was in a series of different and special women-only spaces that I was confronted with my non-fluid, truly Lesbian identity.

As a political feminist, I found that women's spaces helped open my eyes. Feminism is not over. It is important to acknowledge privilege wherever it comes up. I hope that white women will work toward being better allies to women of color. Today, I can take my physical safety and political gains for granted, thanks to the activism of others before I was born. But tomorrow, if I find myself in a different political or cultural environment, where women are not so physically safe, will feminism be "over" in that context?

I believe in acknowledging these simultaneous realities. Today, I am grateful that I do not need to worry about my physical safety from moment to moment. But someday if my life circumstances change for whatever reason, I will take my memories of women's land with me. From women's spaces, I have learned about boundaries. I have learned that I do not need permission from men. I do not need to be who a man tells me to be. I have an internal compass of Lesbian separatism.

I am very lucky that I don't feel the "ache" much anymore. Women's spaces used to feel unattainable. I put them on pedestals. I needed them more than anything to heal, and yet I could not quite grasp at them. Here and there, I had exposure to women's spaces—every time, it was healing and necessary. I am currently someone who feels secure and confident. So when I spend time in women's spaces now, it is just natural, normal, everyday life. I have the luxury of taking these spaces for granted. But I worry that they may be under threat from a political culture that does not understand their necessity.

Is it true that there is a generational divide between Lesbian-feminists? Are younger women not wanting to identify as "Lesbian" (or "lesbian") at all? Are younger women feeling that ache but suppressing it? Maybe there is too much distracting noise for some of these women to pause and listen to the inner ache. This ache is the desire for woman identification. It is the propelling force that could drive younger women toward, not away from, women's land communities.

LESBIAN NATURAL RESOURCES

Rose Norman

One of the mainstays of the Landyke movement since 1991 has been Lesbian Natural Resources (LNR), a nonprofit organization focusing entirely on supporting women's land communities throughout North America. Nett Hart, who was LNR's administrator for many years, reports that LNR remains in business, and emphasizes that "all LNR activity has been done by volunteers, thousands of hours. This has been our greatest resource." [1]

From 1992 through 2000, LNR annually offered two kinds of grants, one for Lesbian land groups that had incorporated as nonprofits (Land Development Grants), and a second category that did not require nonprofit status (Community Development Grants). The grants not requiring nonprofit status supported "accessibility, apprenticeships, economic self-sufficiency, workshops, country skills, networking, community building events, and training for Lesbians and Lesbian communities" or land that "is home to Lesbians/wimmin" or for whom "the intent of the residents is to build Lesbian community." [2] The two kinds of grants were funded through two different organizations, each with its own board. In summer 1999, Tamarack, that year's LNR Coordinator for Grants, provided the following summary in *Maize*:

> Over the first seven years, Land Development Grants have funded $139,900 in down payment grants, $31,400 in mortgages, $61,810 in housing, and $59,278 in development. Community Development Grants have funded $193,496 in accessible living space, visitor buildings, workspaces, tools

1 Quotations from Nett Hart are from email to Rose Norman August 27 and 29, 2014, and a phone interview on August 31, 2014.

2 *Maize* 37 (1993): 29.

and materials for self sufficiency, road repair, community space, skill building workshops, camping area development, community bath houses, greenhouses, passive solar energy, ramps, EI [Environmental Illness] sensitive materials and heating systems, water supplies and garden expansion.[3]

LNR regularly reported grants awarded in the summer issue of *Maize*, starting in 9992 (1992).[4] A review of these *Maize* issues shows that many awards went to Southern land groups, especially for land purchase and for development of cottage industries. Here is how LNR described its goals in *Maize* in 1993:

> The goal of Lesbian Natural Resources is to encourage the sharing of resources in the Lesbian Community so as to encourage autonomous non-patriarchal Lesbian community on land. We recognize the value of land experience and skills as well as money in the materializing of visionary Lesbian community. We encourage Lesbians in North America to participate by applying for grants for projects in your community, encouraging other Lesbian communities to do so, sharing skills you have developed living on land and in self-sustaining cottage industry, and by making and encouraging others to make contributions of money for next year's grants. [5]

Nett Hart says that the money for all these grants comes from "several large donors, many regular donors of all amounts, and bequests [and] . . . many, many small amounts [that] come in, primarily from the communities we funded." The grant committee

---

3   *Maize* 62 (1999): 31.

4   For many years, *Maize* followed the radical feminist practice of numbering years from the birth of agriculture, about 10,000 years ago, believed to have been developed by women. Growing food rather than having to search for it led to the origin of civilization, more significant world-wide than the death of Jesus. In this system, 1992 becomes 9992, for example. Although a common practice among feminists, it apparently disappeared so quickly that few know and understand it now. *Maize* regularized years to common practice after 1999.

5   *Maize* 37 (1993): 29.

for 1997 reported in *Maize* that much of the over $100,000 they awarded that year came from donations of $5 and $10. In addition to grants for land purchase and development, Nett Hart recently pointed out that "concurrent with the grant program we offered advocacy to Landykes in all manner of land and legal areas, providing services of professionals when appropriate. These services saved as many lands as the money. We also funded apprenticeships so Lesbians exploring land community could do so without having to pay or burden the land community."

The last LNR grants list published in *Maize* was in summer 2000. About that time, Hart reports, "the LNR boards realized a need to refocus: not only were we not seeing new, previously unfunded community and individual applicants, most of the lands in our contact were relatively stable financially and legally, and sometimes empty of residents. Outreach to more diverse communities of Lesbians, to areas not networked with other Lesbian lands, and to younger Lesbians became a priority. At the same time it was evident that Lesbian culture was increasingly urban and less attentive to Lesbian/wommon only space across all demographics of Lesbians."

LNR continues to assist Landykes in many ways. For example, they have provided guidance with troubled titles, situations where a titleholder dies intestate and blood relatives become the "owners" of Lesbian land, members leave or, having put money into land, want to get it back, creating messy situations that often lead to losing Lesbian land. One of the long-term projects that LNR has pursued is a resource guide to legal and other issues associated with owning land. In summer 2013, LNR announced the publication of *On Our Own Terms*, "a free resource booklet intended to guide and inspire current and future Landykes. It lists and defines options for the ownership and transfer of Lesbian lands" (p. 66). The legal strategies described here are intended "to provide advocacy and empowerment to Lesbians who are creating and living Lesbian culture on land." LNR provides this book free to

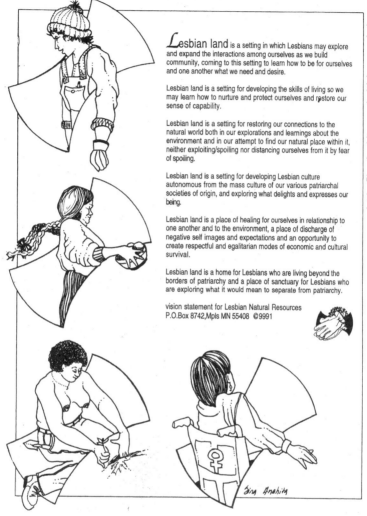

Art by Sine Anahita, used with her permission

*L*esbian land is a setting in which Lesbians may explore and expand the interactions among ourselves as we build community, coming to this setting to learn how to be for ourselves and one another what we need and desire.

Lesbian land is a setting for developing the skills of living so we may learn how to nurture and protect ourselves and restore our sense of capability.

Lesbian land is a setting for restoring our connections to the natural world both in our explorations and learnings about the environment and in our attempt to find our natural place within it, neither exploiting/spoiling nor distancing ourselves from it by fear of spoiling.

Lesbian land is a setting for developing Lesbian culture autonomous from the mass culture of our various patriarchal societies of origin, and exploring what delights and expresses our being.

Lesbian land is a place of healing for ourselves in relationship to one another and to the environment, a place of discharge of negative self images and expectations and an opportunity to create respectful and egalitarian modes of economic and cultural survival.

Lesbian land is a home for Lesbians who are living beyond the borders of patriarchy and a place of sanctuary for Lesbians who are exploring what it would mean to separate from patriarchy.

vision statement for Lesbian Natural Resources
P.O.Box 8742,Mpls MN 55408 ©9991

LNR Vision Statement, published in *Maize* and widely distributed.

Lesbians. Orders are fulfilled through *Maize*: PO Box 240, Serafina, NM 87569, or email JaeHaggard@gmail.com, and provide name, land name (if any), and mailing address. Write to LNR at Lesbian Natural Resources, PO Box 8742, Minneapolis, MN 55408.

WOMEN'S LAND IN SOUTHERN STATES
Kate Ellison

This listing of fifty-one women's land groups in eleven Southern states began with Pelican Lee's list of womyn's land groups across the nation.[1] This list grew out of a slide show that Shewolf developed during her travels to women's lands. Shewolf brought her slide projector and showed the slide show wherever she could—at womyn's bookstores, community centers—and later showed them regularly at Landyke Gatherings. The list (and the definition of "women's land") has been a moving target. We expanded the list using three issues of *Shewolf's Directory* (1994–95, 1997–98, 2013–16),[2] the *Maize 2014 Connections & Resources Directory*,[3] and individual women's memories. The focus is on intentional community and creating alternatives. Some listings are womyn who live rurally by ones and twos, and many campgrounds have no or few permanent residents.

The symbol "♀" before a listing indicates lands with essays, memoirs, or interviews in this issue.

---

1 Pelican's list is unpublished, but see also Pelican Lee, "Setting Up Women's Land in the 1970s: Could We Do It?" *off our backs* (March–April 2003): 43–47.

2 While intentional communities like Twin Oaks (since 1967, in Virginia), Earthhaven (since 1994, in western North Carolina), and Dancing Rabbit Ecovillage (since 1997, in Missouri) are listed in *Shewolf's Directory*, and are still in existence and welcoming Lesbians, they are not set up as women-only land, so we have not included them in our listing. See http://www.ic.org/. One exception was Peacemaker Land Trust, which was not Lesbian-owned but was an early attempt to start a Lesbian land group by radical feminists who questioned the owning of land, and believed in the land trust philosophy. That land trust philosophy is explained by Mildred J. Loomis, "A Practice in Social Change," *Henry George News*, February 1970, online at http://www.cooperativeindividualism.org/loomis-mildred_a-practice-in-social-change-1970.html. The land is held in trust and is not "reconvertible into property."

3 *Maize* 108 (Winter 2013–14): 10–23.

Peacemaker Land Trust womyn standing on the sill of the cabin they are
building on land in West Virginia, early 1970s.
(l to r) Lillian Willoughby (Sally Willowbee's mother, who was visiting),
Janet, Harvest, Gigi, Nita, Mel, and Sally.

1969 In Gainesville, Florida, Corky Culver and other members
of her Lesbian consciousness-raising group form a women's
land group and start searching for land to buy.

1971–73 *Peacemaker Land Trust*—Small farm near Hinton, West
Virginia. Coming out of the nonviolent peace movement,
which included the land trust movement and the feminist
movement, and after picking apples together on an all-
women's apple picking crew, four women moved to West
Virginia to live on the Peacemaker Land Trust. Two more
women joined, and they started building a cabin on the land
and growing vegetables. Several women came out there.
Unable to find jobs, they moved on, some to live on other
women's land.

♀ 1972–present *The North Forty* (aka *Long Leaf*)—Forty acres
in north-central Florida, purchased by an intentional group
(including Corky Culver) as affordable land for Lesbians,
with skills sharing, gatherings, and community.

♀ 1974–present *Dragon/DW Outpost*—A 132-acre residential
community in southern Missouri, eco-friendly subsistence
living, not looking to add members, and plenty of camping
space.

♀ 1975–present *Belly Acres*—Merril Mushroom, author, networker, and Lesbian activist, made her home here. With radical fairie husband, she adopted and raised five hard-to-place, mostly mixed-race children on land in rural Middle Tennessee.

♀ 1976–1980 *Sassafras*—Begun in 1972 as a group of men and women on 500 rugged acres in the Arkansas Ozarks, they first transitioned to women's community (1976), and then gradually donated most of the acreage to women of color, now Arco Iris.

♀ 1976–present *Sugarloaf Women's Village*—On Sugarloaf Key, fifteen miles northeast of Key West, Florida, six lots, with four houses, a small guesthouse, and smaller "chalet," this is now an active vacation and camping destination, with four residents.

♀ 1977–present *Arco Iris*—Begun by Maria (then known as Sun Hawk, now Águila) on 120 rugged acres adjacent to Sassafras

Rear view of Sugarloaf community house,
a screen porch now converted to a bedroom.

in northern Arkansas, as sanctuary for women and children of color, especially indigenous women. Eventually, two parcels were added, to total 530 acres, most as protected wilderness. See earthcareproject.wordpress.com.

♀ 1977–present *Pagoda*—This seaside group of twelve small cottages and two larger buildings in St. Augustine, Florida, offered Lesbian-only homes and active community building until the 1990s, including frequent concerts, art exhibits, workshops, and feminist process.

1978–1988 *Okra Ridge Natural Laboratory*—Intentional community started by Catherine Risingflame, Boone, and others on 100 acres of valley surrounded by ridges, near Oak Ridge, Tennessee. Central house with amenities and four simple private living spaces scattered around the mostly wooded land.

♀ 1978–1985 *Turtleland* —Twenty acres of secluded woodland, with a creek on one border, in northern Virginia. Camping,

By Amanda Clements Butler, used with her permission

As conflict within Turtleland overwhelmed hope, Mandy created this etching, a testimony to the dream of Lesbian land. Housemate to Jes, Kate, and Toni, Mandy was close with everyone in the collective and lived the struggle almost as much as the members.

ceremonies, music. Active collective of five wimmin, 1981–1984.

1979–present *Swiftwaters*—Near Dahlonega, Georgia, started as a riverside resort/weekend camp with cabins and tent space for Lesbians, now for women and children, www.swiftwaters.com.

1980–present *Greentree*—Lesbian land in the Missouri Ozarks adjoining Dragon. For twenty-two years home to Mosa (Mimi Baczewska).

1981–1987 *Whypperwillow*—320 acres of very secluded open womyn's land in a beautiful valley in the Arkansas Ozarks. Three womyn-built dwellings, a barn and shed renovated for dwellings, drinkable hand pump and spring box, no electricity. Financial issues around the land mortgage led to a lawsuit that split the land and ultimately ended the community.

♀ 1981–present *Maud's Land/OLHA* (Ozark Land Holding Association)—280 acres northwest of Fayetteville, Arkansas. Starting with twenty memberships, there are now twelve on the land, with five living nearby.

♀ 1981–present *SPIRAL*—290 wooded acres in south-central Kentucky, home to about fifteen Lesbians over time, creating intentional community, building houses, a large organic garden, and a campground.

♀ 1982–present *Silver Circle Sanctuary*—Forty acres near Holly Springs, Mississippi, home to three Lesbians, four dwellings, outbuildings, gardening, and wildlife.

1983 *Maize: A Lesbian Country Magazine* begins publication, then based in New York, now in New Mexico, PO Box 130, Serafina, NM 87569.

1983–present *Cedar Hollow*—Forty-two acres in a land trust in southern Kentucky. Home to two and sometimes more Lesbians living off the grid until 2006. Since then, one house and guest space have electricity. Two dwellings remain off the grid, one with active solar. Permaculture farming, with orchards, ponds, woods, three dwellings. Apprenticeship in simple living, chainsaw construction, organic gardening.

♀ 1983–present *Pteradyktil* (aka *Sandhill Farm*)—Seventy-two acres of wooded and open land in east Georgia with house, cabins, community house, and pool.

♀ 1984–present *WIT's End Farm*—This 100 acres adjacent to Belly Acres in Tennessee was the site of the July 4th Unfinished Revolution, where Lesbians gathered yearly to celebrate continuing to be American revolutionaries. Main house and barn, stream bed, sloping fields, and steeper woods. Sold to a Lesbian in her forties in 2014, and renamed Pounce Farm.

1985–present *The Mound/Sweet Haven*—Lesbian land with two houses and two cabins in the Missouri Ozarks, adjoining Greentree, near Dragon.

1985–2010 *Bold Moon*—Sine Anahita lived on twenty-one acres of woods, meadow, and riverfront near Greensboro, North Carolina, for fourteen years with and without others, for camping and hosting women's events. In 2008, it was donated to the Guilford County green space program, which has since added thirty-one acres and maintains it as wilderness, known as Bold Moon Preserve. During her time on that land, Anahita published at least fifteen issues of *The Womyn on the Land Network* newsletter.

♀ 1985–2011 *Gathering Root*—Eighty acres in southern Missouri, old farmhouse, creek, established organic gardens.

♀ 1985–2002 *Womonworld* (aka *Woman's World*)—Shewolf's 100 acres of bottomland about forty minutes north of New Orleans, Louisiana. Large tent gatherings were held in 1993, 1995, and 1996, focused on construction skills, yurt building, and community.

1986–present *Laughing Eagle*—Twenty acres in north-central Florida, with three to four residents and many visitors.

Corky Culver working in a neighbor's hayfield, 1975.

Organic garden, main house, geodesic dome, and a cottage. Not seeking new residents, but visitors welcome with planning. Cate and Kirsten.

1986–present *Moonhaven*—Small shady farm near Santa Fe Lake in north-central Florida, home of animal communicator and astrologer Flash Silvermoon, and her partner Pandora Lightmoon, both musicians, plus many animals. The scene of many Rainbow Goddess Circles for the Holidays, and many healing sessions. Flash teaches classes and created the Wise Woman's Festival, held for eight years.

1987–2011 *Something Special*—Off I-95 in a residential area in Miami, Florida, this was "Miami's only Lesbian-owned and operated, wimmin only gathering space." Backyard camping, dinner in Maryanne and F. Louise's home, multicultural neighborhood.

1987–present *Cedar Hill*—Radical lesbian-feminists Paula Mariedaughter and Jeanne Neath have lived at Cedar

Hill since 1987 on forty-three remote acres of Arkansas hardwood forest with an organic garden. Camping. Their blog is The Cedar Hill Report: Ecofeminism, Subsistence Living and Nature Awareness at www.ecofeminismblog.org.

♀ 1988–present *Full Circle Farm*—120 acres south of Chapel Hill, North Carolina. Lynn Hicks now shares the land with ten adults and four children (half living there full-time), who have bought parcels. An old farmhouse, barn, sheds, log cabin, and new homes.

1988–present *Somerset Farm*—162 acres of West Virginia's mountainous forest, hay fields, and rolling pasture, with house and barns, secluded yet accessible to the highway. Judy Winsett, a Lesbian jeweler, lives here with two horses, room for more. Campers and visitors welcome, and the possibility of creating a land trust.

1988–present *The Whimsy*—Between Fort Lauderdale and Miami, Florida, 1.25 acres, for travelers who can camp, RV, or stay in guest-house. Political and cultural activism.

♀ 1989–present *Hawk Hill Community Land Trust*—Lesbian land trust, part of a 3000-acre land trust in the Missouri Ozarks.

1989–2000 *Merry Macha*—Fifteen acres in the mountains of western North Carolina, started by Sharon Bienert and Pam Guthrie. They converted a barn to a house for women-only nightly and weekly rental from 1991 until 2000. Ran daylily nursery from 1993 to 1999, with a grant for two years from LNR to host apprentices.

1990–92 *Cloudland*—The women-owned land used for the first three years of Rhythmfest (1990–92), a women's music festival featuring music, art, and politics. In north Georgia, rolling hills and fields, near Alabama, used mostly as a girls' horseback riding ranch.

♀ 1990–present *Womontown*—In midtown Kansas City, Missouri, an urban, seven square block residential area where low-cost houses and apartment buildings were individually purchased or rented by more than seventy-five

Lesbians and renovated to create a diverse oasis from a blighted neighborhood.

♀ 1991–present *Lesbian Natural Resources* begins awarding cash grants for purchase, down payment, improvement, apprenticeships, and many other uses, in support of developing Lesbian land communities. Based in Minneapolis, Minnesota, and still in business through a PO Box; first advertised in *Maize* in 1991: PO Box 8742, Minneapolis, MN 55408.

LNR logo as published in Maize #67 (2000).

♀ 1993–present *Camp Sister Spirit*—120 acres, near Ovett, Mississippi. Brenda and Wanda Henson started this as a site for the Gulf Coast Women's Festival, and for years offered camping and other activities, until they got national publicity after a spell of homophobic harassment. Brenda died in 2008, and the land is now unoccupied.

1993–present *Ravens Den Sanctuary*—Six Lesbians bought 100 acres outside of Sewanee, Tennessee in 1993. A seventh joined in 1997, one was bought out (at the cost of five acres), and in 2013, the remaining six donated the 95 acres to the South Cumberland Regional Land Trust (SCRLT), retaining the right to live and build on the land under the terms of a lease with SCRLT and a conservation easement registered in 2007 with Tennessee Parks and Greenways. One woman lives on the land.

♀ 1993 *Shewolf's Directory of Wimmin's Lands*, first edition. In small type under the large title was "and Lesbian Communities," and the dates 1994–95 (though printed in 1993). Contact: PO Box 1515, Melrose, FL 32666 or email wimminland@aol.com.

1994–present *CampOut* (originally *In Touch*)—Between Richmond and Charlottesville, Virginia, 96 acres, open first weekend in April to end of October; Virginia Women's Music Festival held here in spring, as well as many other festivals and gatherings in the past.

1994–present *Spinsterhaven*—An intentional group of women formed in 1988, focused on aging, purchased forty-three wooded acres in Madison County, Arkansas, in 1994. The land was sold in 2014.

Photo by Jacque Allen, used with permission

Deerheart dining hall at Camp Pleiades, "where we ate a lot of meals, drank a lot of wine and had a lot of fun," writes co-owner Jacque Allen.

1995–2005 *Camp Pleiades*—A Lesbian camp in western North Carolina, run by Jacque and Barbara, who also owned A1A Funwear (clothing sold at festivals). They sold the property in 2014 to a conservancy.

1996–present *Carefree Resort*—The Resort on Carefree Boulevard, northern Fort Myers, Florida; fifty acres with 278 manufactured homes and RV lots; "Southwest Florida's premier Lesbian destination"; 130 full-time residents (http://www.resortoncb.com/).

1996–2000 *Full Moon Farm*—Located forty miles north of Womonworld in Louisiana, provided a safe haven and retreat for Lesbian interracial couples and friends, with a large house on private wooded land with a lake.

♀ 1997–present *Alapine Village*—In northeast Alabama near the Georgia line, a community of forty-five individually owned two-acre lots (fifteen developed). Some residents formed the Alapine Community Association, and one of the focuses is on aging in place. Founded by women who moved from The Pagoda.

1997–present *Wisperwood*—Fifty-five acres in central Kentucky, home to two Lesbians. Two pastures, rolling wooded hills, a stream, two outbuildings, and a house. Fruit trees, raspberries, blueberries, and blackberries.

1998–present *Avalon Farms*—A Lesbian-owned horse farm on 300 acres northwest of Nashville, offering boarding, horse training, and lessons on site. Practices natural horsemanship principles (one owner, Val, is a level 3 Parelli student). Primitive camping (no hookups). For info, contact valerie@avalonfarmblog.com.

♀ 1998–present *Maat Dompim*—In Virginia near Appomattox. Owned by a tax-exempt organization working since 1992 to establish a facility reflecting women-of-color values.

1999–2001 *SHELL*—Supportive Healing Environment of Long-Living Lesbians, a serious attempt to build an accessible senior living space on sixteen acres on Lookout Mountain in northeast Alabama. Three buildings were constructed, and some womyn lived there, but the land has been sold and the buildings moved.

2000–present *Poco-A-Poco Farm*—One-and-a-quarter-acre homestead, twenty-minute drive from Appalachian Trail in West Virginia. Harvest currently lives there, with an organic garden, herbs, native perennials.

Drawing by Harvest, used with her permission

Campfire cooking in the 1970s.

2000–present *Siren Song*—Six and a half acres with several dwellings and huge oak trees, between Ocala and Gainesville, Florida, presently for sale.

2000–present *Swamp Dance*—Twelve acres, including a pond, at the tip of the Ocala National Forest, Florida. Home to Pat High and her partner, volunteers, and apprentices, living off the grid, building Native American structures, creating lapidary art particularly with meteorites, kayaking, teaching classes. Removing invasive plants, farming with native plants and shiitake mushrooms, using biological insect control, solar-powered irrigation.

2007– present *Lofty Notions*—Rents out a single-site campsite (RV or tents) in Rutherfordton, North Carolina, 35 miles southeast of Asheville. This single, private campsite overlooks a beautiful 12-foot waterfall and has water, sewer, and electric (30 amp), loftynotions1@yahoo.com

2012–present *Lake Annie Womonspace*—Lakefront lot in north-central Florida, home of Jenna, Wirth, and frequent visitors. Several living spaces, workshop, office, dock.

Lesbian Lands Southeast, Alphabetical

Alapine Village

Arco Iris

Avalon Farms

Belly Acres

Bold Moon

Camp Pleiades

Camp Sister Spirit

CampOut

Carefree Resort

Cedar Hill

Cedar Hollow

Cloudland

Dragon/DW Outpost

Full Circle Farm

Full Moon Farm

Gathering Root

Greentree

Hawk Hill Community
    Land Trust

In Touch

Lake Annie Womonspace

Laughing Eagle

Lofty Notions

Long Leaf (North Forty)

Maat Dompim

Maud's Land (OLHA)

Merry Macha

Moonhaven

North Forty

Okra Ridge Natural Laboratory

OLHA

Pagoda

Peacemaker Land Trust

Poco-A-Poco Farm

Pounce Farm (WIT's End Farm)

Pteradyktil

Ravens Den Sanctuary

Sandhill Farm (Pteradyktil)

Sassafras

SHELL

Silver Circle Sanctuary

Siren Song

Sister Spirit (Camp Sister Spirit)

Somerset Farm

Something Special

Spinsterhaven

SPIRAL

Sugarloaf Women's Village

Swamp Dance

Swiftwaters

The Mound/Sweet Haven

The Whimsy

Turtleland

Whypperwillow

Wisperwood

WIT's End Farm

Woman's World (Womonworld)

Womontown

Womonworld

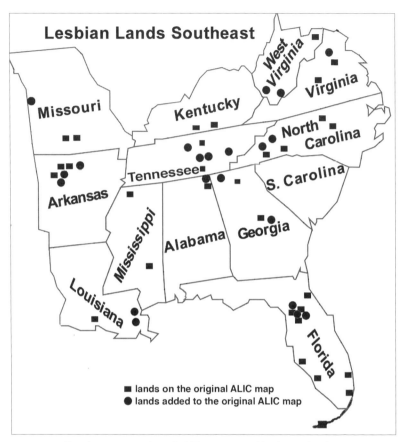

Southeastern portion of a US map created by Jessey Ina-Lee
to show approximate locations of women's lands, part of a project
done by ALIC (Association of Lesbians in Community) in the early 2000s.
Locations are approximate, and sometimes several land groups are indicated
by one square when they are close together. Squares
were on original map; dots were added, indicated by italics in legend.

Drawing used with permission of Jessey Ina-Lee, cropped and edited by Rand Hall, with
content assistance from Pelican Lee, Rose Norman, Merril Mushroom, and Kate Ellison

Lesbian Lands Southeast

ALABAMA
Alapine
SHELL

ARKANSAS
?Apple Acres
Cedar Hill
*Cross Creek
OLHA/Maud's Land
Rancho Arco Iris
Sassafras
Spinsterhaven
Whypperwillow

FLORIDA
Carefree
Lake Annie
Womonspace
Laughing Eagle
Moonhaven
North Forty (Long Leaf)
Pagoda
?Palms of Manasota
Siren Song
Something Special
Sugarloaf Women's Village
Swamp Dance
Whimsy

GEORGIA
Cloudland
?Pine Woods Colony
Pteradyktil
Swiftwaters

KENTUCKY
Cedar Hollow
SPIRAL
Wisperwood

LOUISIANA
?Les Femmes Deux
Full Moon Farm
Womonworld (Woman's World)

MISSISSIPPI
Camp Sister Spirit
Silver Circle Sanctuary

MISSOURI
Dragon
Gathering Root
Greentree
Hawk Hill
The Mound/ Sweet Haven
Womontown

NORTH CAROLINA
Bold Moon
Camp Pleiades
Full Circle
Merry Macha
Lofty Notions
?Makarow of Charlotte

TENNESSEE
Avalon Farms
Belly Acres
?Turkey Branch
Okra Ridge Natural Lab
Raven's Den Sanctuary
WIT's End Farm

VIRGINIA
Camp Out (In Touch)
Maat Dompim
Turtleland

WEST VIRGINIA
Peacemaker Land Trust
Poco-A-Poco Farm
Somerset Farm

*Cross Creek is the informal name for a collection of separate, private, small landholdings, mostly held by Lesbians/women, across the creek from OLHA.
? Rural, Lesbian-owned land groups from the original map that appeared in Shewolf's Landyke slide show at one time, but about which we have no information. Some may be B&B's or campgrounds.

LESBIANA:
A PARALLEL REVOLUTION (FILM REVIEW)
Reviewed by Barbara Esrig

A documentary film by Myriam Fougère
(Canada, 2012, 63 min. Available from Groupe Intervention
Video, http://www.givideo.org/ or email info@givideo.org.)

> *Lesbiana. It became my country, a space where I belonged.*
> *A territory beyond borders made up of islands linked to each*
> *other by love, ideas, and political affinities.*
> Myriam Fougère, from *Lesbiana*

> *You know when you're living in it, you don't realize you're*
> *making history, until after it's over. . .* Carol V. Moore, from
> *Lesbiana*

If there is one Lesbian documentary that you should see to really understand what the peak of the Lesbian-feminist movement looked like, felt like, spoke like, and, indeed, was like, between the mid-1970s, and early 1990s, *Lesbiana* is *that* quintessential film. This film chronicles how, spawned from the womyn's movement, the need for womyn-only space and Lesbian separatist space became more and more evident and paramount for many of the radical thinkers.

If you were there, it will be so familiar that you might see womyn you know (or even yourself!). If you weren't there but always wished you had been and wanted to have an experience (albeit a vicarious one) of what Lesbian culture was like back then, this will do it!

Myriam Fougère, a Québécoise Lesbian, artist, filmmaker, archivist, and traveler by design, spent much time during the

1980s traveling up and down the East Coast, as far west as Texas, as far south as Florida, living in her van and seeking radical communities in both Canada and the United States, meeting, living, and loving these Lesbians who were creating womyn-only space. This documentary, which was narrated, shot, directed, and edited by her alone, documents her return, decades later, with archival video recordings and dozens of interviews with many of these womyn whom she had known: artists, musicians, writers, academics, all political activists in their own right, and, indeed, mothers of the movement. They talk about what it meant and why it was important to create a place that embodied Lesbian culture, politics, and their own Lesbian identity.

Creating Lesbian space, however, did not mean that everything was always copacetic (ask any radical feminist who was living in the front lines!), and the tellers touch on this too. *Lesbiana* then is a film, a forum, of womyn telling their real stories, describing the best of times and the trying times. While womyn speak of how extraordinary their lives were, the immense safety and nurturing there was living in a construct that they had created, and providing a dream and a politic that has remained to this very day, they also speak of the difficulties. It makes us groan remembering as others tell of how strangely narrow and restrictive their community could become, the endless processing of what was politically correct or incorrect, the importance of words and consensus and the endless theoretical dialectic and Lesbian ideology of how things "really" were. So many independent womyn, all with lots of ideas that, as it turned out, were not always compatible.

But what Fougère does so extraordinarily skillfully and heart-fully in *Lesbiana* is touch us deeply in remembering the courage, the will, the character of that period: a zeitgeist that had a spirit like no other. It was our school, we were each other's teachers, and as hard or easy as it was for those who lived during those decades, the irrevocable truth is that none of us would be who we are "if it wasn't for the women, women/we would not be living, living/we would not be joyful singing/Loving and beloved womyn."[1]

Cover photo from the film *Lesbiana* (2012).

Lesbiana is only an hour long, but it's a journey into our past that you won't want to miss. It's the kind of film that deserves a movie theater filled with young and old dykes for a great evening. In fact, have a potluck, invite all your friends over, and it will be the most fun you've had in a very long time.

> **Parallel Revolution:** "Instead of fighting against patriarchy, we created a parallel world. Parallel is something that exists alongside and in the margins. We tried to create a whole universe that was beside this one instead of transforming this one. I did not want to fight to create change. It was too negative. We did not have a minute to lose. . . . We wanted to create a different world based on what we wanted and dreamed of."[2]

Lesbiana includes both English and French speakers and is subtitled when necessary. It has been shown in over fifty film festivals and theaters around the world.

---

1 From Alix Dobkin's song "If It Wasn't For The Women," from her album *Alix Dobkin: Love & Politics, A 30-Year Saga* (1992), Women's Wax Works A007, Mfg. by Ladyslipper Music, Inc., Durham, NC.

2 From Rose Norman's interview with Myriam Fougère, conducted at Myriam's Pagoda cottage in St. Augustine, Florida, January 29, 2013.

BOOK REVIEW

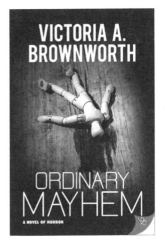

Ordinary Mayhem
by **Victoria A. Brownworth**
Bold Strokes Books
ISBN: 978-1626393158
Paperback $16.95, 264 pages

Reviewed by Caely McHale

Author Victoria A. Brownworth declares *Ordinary Mayhem* to be a "novel of horror" beneath the haunting image of a bloody wooden form sprawled across the cover of her latest book. I opened the book with anticipation, expecting to find the stuff of Hollywood bone chillers--vampires around the corner and ghosts slamming doors in the night. Instead, Brownworth describes a different kind of horror through the story of her tortured protagonist, Faye Blakemore.

Faye has a dark passion for the macabre in her photojournalism and a deeply hidden secret, one that has shaped her life from the time she lost her parents to a burning car when she was six years old. As her story unfolds across the varying landscapes of her grandparent's house in Brooklyn, St. Cecilia's Home for Girls, the streets of Manhattan and the violent roads of the Democratic Republic of Congo (DRC), readers are brought face to face with the true horror of the book--the shocking violence and cruelty of which humankind is capable.

Written in a series of fleeting and interwoven snapshots of Faye's dark past and troubled present, the disturbing narrative unfolds. Faye became a ward of the state at 10 when she confessed to a nun at St. Cecilia's that her grandfather, "Grand", had been horrifically killing and mutilating women in his basement, and chronicling his "artwork" with photographs. As Faye grows up to become a celebrated photojournalist, she carries with her the guilt of her grandfather's homicidal past, and the fear that one day he might return for her.

The title *Ordinary Mayhem* is repeatedly examined and defined in the book, lodged in the mind of Faye as she travels the world in search of women's stories that need to be told. "She wanted to tell her stories, but she never wanted to be perceived as a monster just because she wanted to roll back the rock to see what slithered underneath... Faye didn't create the things no one wanted to see-and it wasn't because of her people couldn't keep themselves from looking." Ordinary Mayhem can be found within every living person. Ordinary Mayhem is not the evil deed done by the fairy tale villain, but the elderly man next door or the bagger at the grocery store. Ordinary Mayhem can be grotesque and shocking, like the violent rapes and attacks Faye chronicles when she visits the DRC, or it can be the invisible and insidious seed of fear in the heart of a child.

What Brownworth does so skillfully in *Ordinary Mayhem* is walk on the thin line between the unbearable image and the necessary pain of visualizing it. Much like Faye, Brownworth seeks to roll back the rock and uncover a startling picture of the violence of which all humans are capable. Brownworth looks and looks hard because the only way ordinary mayhem can be stopped is by the grim acknowledgement of its reality.

Stroppy Dykes by **Jean Taylor**
Dyke Books Inc.
ISBN: 978-0-9806261-1-7
Paperback $40, 872 pages

Reviewed by Caely McHale

In *Stroppy Dykes*, Jean Taylor narrates feminist and lesbian actions and spaces in Victoria and the effects the 1980s movement had on Australian aboriginal and islander women—women whose stories are often omitted from the traditional story of lesbian activism. With an outstanding level of sensitivity and care, Taylor brings to life the lesbian and feminist scene of Australia.

A driving force within the book is the need for lesbians to band together and retain a common identity through organizations and gathering spaces during a time of social change. Sometimes reading like a diary, sometimes like a newsletter, and even occasionally like a textbook outlining point by the point the important historical moment of an era, *Stroppy Dykes* is an incredible feat of research. In her introduction, Jean Taylor apologizes that she had to cut more than 500 pages, leaving out some meetings and events. Personally, I could not imagine a more detailed and complete rendering of an entire decade of activity.

While the scope of the book is daunting, Taylor is able to inject the facts and dates with lightness and familiarity through pairing snippets of her own life in the community with illuminating quotes and descriptions of feminist and lesbian events and groups. The diary effect grounds the book in a place of emotional investment for the reader, and in a way Taylor acts as the pseudo-protagonist of the book. Her cast of characters broadens to include moments with lovers, family, friends, and colleagues. A treat for the reader at the end of each section of the book is interviews and profiles of lesbian women Taylor met in her experiences with the Victoria lesbian community. The voices of these women are stark, intense, funny, and personal. In a few pages, readers find out how these women came out, who they fell in and out of love with, the activism they were involved in, their successes, and even their failures. Like sitting down for story time at the foot of a wise woman, each interview is a fruitful and intimate moment.

Thanks to Jean Taylor's amazing attention to detail when chronicling her lesbian community, not only local meetings and actions are discussed. The book is also a surprising resource not only for history but also for forgotten movies, books, and poetry that made an impact in the 1980s, especially in Australia. *Stroppy Dykes* will lead readers to many interesting books and websites about the Victoria community. The addicting nature of the search for information exudes from Taylor and infects readers; the quest to preserve lesbian herstory continues.

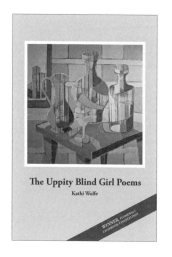

The Uppity Blind Girl Poems
Kathi Wolfe

Uppity Blind Girl by **Kathi Wolfe**
BrickHouse Books, Inc
ISBN: 978-1938144271
Paperback $12, 42 pages

Reviewed by Caely McHale

*U*ppity *Blind Girl* is a joyful escape from reality into the alter ego of author Kathi Wolfe. Other reviewers describe the character "Uppity" as the popular and vibrant girl you wanted to be friends with at school, with her wise one-liners and vibrant collection of shining shoes. Together, Wolfe and Uppity illuminate the world of the blind and the world of the lesbian through short passages of unadulterated thoughtfulness with an emphasis on perspective.

The first poem of the chapbook, "Happy Hour," sets the tone by convincing the reader that being blind is the easy way out; seeing is not a privilege but a burden. While this may be a difficult concept, Wolfe delivers it with humor and clarity. "*Am I getting chubby?* Uppity averts / her gaze from the bar's green, moldy walls. / *Am I going gray at 22? Would I kiss / anyone with zits? Or less than perfect abs?*"

"The Planet of the Blind" describes a world without traditional sight in deliciously sensory and seductive terms. "*Mirrors are for aliens*, Uppity said. / *The sun tastes like red velvet cake; / your lover's voice is a cashmere cape; / a clown's smile smells of orange blossom / and ashes. You are your own shadow.*" Each image is both shockingly true and strikingly foreign to a sight-abled reader. These poems showcase Wolfe's gift to see far beyond the ordinary of this world and then deliver her version back to us, who can only see the sun as light.

Wolfe's knack for sharp and sexy imagery carries throughout the book. In "ScentsSpeakeasy.com: Blogspot, "Uppity writes to the editor of the website to answer a question about her blindness in connection with the rest of her senses. In a flash of what is simultaneously sharp derision and delicate soul searching, Uppity declares "Tin eared scribe, your vision / blinds you. Can you see / if a beer tastes like rubies / or smells like unwashed hair? / Unhitched from eyes, I devour secrets."

Beneath the quick jokes and beautiful sensations, there remains a dark undertone of satire. In "Blind Porn," Wolfe tells the story of Uppity and her lover Sabrina, kissing in Washington Square Park, only to be objectified and fetishized by a passing male, for their shared blindness as well as their gayness. The sadness of the title is gripping, illuminating the connection between what so many understand as harmless voyeurism in viewing porn and how that same objectifying power of women can cross from the screen to the street in an instant. However, Uppity holds her head high, aims, and fires back at the man--a "fury in spiked heels." As the poem concludes, a self-reflective dialogue is introduced between Uppity and Wolfe.

"Why, to the sighted,
are we creatures
from the Black Lagoon?
Uppity wondered.
They turn off the TV,
undress,
sip wine,
check their breath,
pray to the gods
of good sex
and tenderness,
just as I do now before making love
to my lady."

Used to this life of otherness, Uppity rejects the notion that porn and disability have to be a bad and dirty thing in the context of her own life; if she is viewed and commented, she will carry on and enjoy it. "If this be blind porn, / play on."

I Remind Myself...:
Selected Poetry
by Ruth Mountaingrove

Reviewed by Caely McHale

Ruth Mountaingrove's collection of selected poetry *I Remind Myself...* contains a loose narrative of self-discovery punctuated by Mountaingrove's fast paced stanzas and images that ring stunningly true to life. *I Remind Myself...* emanates a sense of feeling before thinking and planning, organic words following one after another like speaking in a dream.

The poem, "This old lesbian dreams," paints a fantasy image of a lover for the older speaker of the poem. Without frills, the wants and needs are solid. "This old / lesbian, who can have any / women she can imagine / dreams this dyke, black / trousers, fancy top, with radiant / face, holding her, kissing her." The poem speaks to the issue of female aging and the urgent sense of desire that remains behind from youth. However, the speaker ends the poem alone. Like many of the poems in the collection, the speaker is perceiving and dreaming but not present.

The same feeling of concrete, hands-on desire appears in "How to Wash a Silk Shirt". The love is methodic, simple and physical in a way that shows deep connection and caring: "kiss the woman / next to you. Soap her / just as you did your silk shirt. / Her arms. her breasts. her back. / Turn on the shower, rinse well, / turning her in your arms." Similarly, "Strawberries" weighs in with delicate and almost shameful intimacy, naked to the world. "As I rounded the corner / there she was / naked to the morning, / to the strawberries, / and to me."

The most powerful poem in the "Medical Septet" section is titled "Prelude." Putting into abstract terms the experience of a male medical practitioner touching the body of a lesbian, touch becomes a different beast. "Spreading jelly / under my breasts, / touching my skin. / We could be lovers, / his head so close to mine." However, the illusion of intimacy is broken by machinery and reality; this interaction is not natural and soft like "Strawberries".

It exists in a different realm of necessity and a lack of power. However, the reader is left wondering, is this environment somehow emotionally safer for the speaker? "He knows my heart's / secrets. / He does not kiss me / He does not / betray my heart."

"Observations" is the last section of the collection. The speaker seems tired, tense and agitated. The haunting poem, "Question" follows the same staccato rhythm of this final section, asking the question. "When / you / lie / in bed / waiting / for / dawn / who / waits / with / you?" The aloneness of the lines on the page feels like solidarity—or imagined solidarity.

The final poem in Mountaingrove's collection, "Holidaze," contains playful wordplay and rhyme contrasting with the melancholy nature of the piece. The collection artfully comes in full circle. "My muse is not amused. She keeps knocking on my door / but I'm ignoring her.... She has much to say / I need to listen." *I Remind Myself...* ends with a bittersweet taste. The speaker is not alone, the speaker has and has always had poetry to sustain herself. Mountaingrove carefully illustrates to the experience of a lesbian living life after explosions of youth and desire and danger. What remains is a well of wisdom running deeper than the need for abstract conceits or high-flying metaphor, and a stunningly discerning eye for what life is.

HOPE: Newfound Clarity
by **Pat M. Kuras**
CreateSpace
ISBN: 978-1511577205
Paperback $9.99, 34 pages

Reviewed by Caely McHale

In the author's note preceding *Hope: Newfound Clarity*, Pat Kuras states "Writing is an act of discovery and I write to understand and make sense of the world around me." Following the poetic narrative of redemption, *Hope* delivers tight poetic imagery and a language that proudly display's the speaker's heart on her sleeve as she battles alcoholism.

Standouts from the collection include the poem "The St. Valentine's Day Massacre," in which the speaker refers to a "kamikaze flight" as she anxiously searches for a human connection under the thick veil of inebriation. Longing comes through delicately in the line "I dive from woman to woman, / pressing petals, lips to lips, / kisses that are, oh, too brief" and then fades into artistic oblivion with the poem's final assertion, "Like a Van Gogh night, / I am lost to a swirl of colors."

Lines from one of the final poems, "Recovery," capture best the spirit of Kuras' endeavor in this collection. "You were blinded before / powerless against the / wicked nectars." At the end, the poet finds "A newfound clarity, / the promise of new days and progress not perfection."

CONTRIBUTORS

B. Leaf Cronewrite is Maryann Hopper's crone name. She grew up in Mississippi, and graduated from Arkansas Tech and the University of Memphis. Activism caused her to join marches protesting violence against women in Memphis, supporting Lesbian and gay rights in Washington, DC, and Pride marches in many cities. With her partner, Drea Firewalker, she created an intentional women's urban community named Womontown within her 7 × 7 block neighborhood in Kansas City, Missouri.

Barbara Ester grew up in the country in Illinois and holds a great affinity for Lesbians on Land. A *Maize* reader and writer for many years, she now resides in South Carolina, living on the forest edge.

Barbara Hering Lieu was born in New York State and has lived in the South and in Lesbian community since the late 1970s, first at Pagoda in St. Augustine, Florida, and currently at Alapine Village in northeast Alabama.

Dolphin Dragon grew up in West Texas, taught school and made movies in Chicago, and attended the second Michigan Womyn's Music Festival. There she was handed a life-changing flier, which led her to the Ozarks and Dragon, where she found love and learned a lot.

Drea Firewalker is Andrea Nedelsky's crone name. Drea graduated from UMKC (1984). She was a security marshal in the first Pride marches in Kansas City. The need to help secure a strong community for Lesbians prompted her and her partner, B. Leaf Cronewrite, to lead a movement to transform an area in the Longfellow/Dutch Hill neighborhood, which became known as Womontown, Missouri, and still exists today.

Jenna Weston is an artist, writer, and teacher. She grew up in Michigan and came out there in the late 1970s. Since then Jenna has been committed to the creation of Lesbian community and culture, contributing her art and writing to numerous women's and Lesbian publications. She now lives in north Florida.

Juana Maria Paz is a New York-born Puerto Rican who spent several years living on Lesbian land and writing about feminist community. She is currently a child care worker in Richmond, Virginia, and lives with her daughter and grandson.

Judy McVey was born in Columbia, South Carolina, and raised in Chattanooga, Tennessee, and Atlanta, Georgia. She is a retired orchestra teacher and pastoral counselor and is now living out her dream with her partner of thirty-one years on their land in east Georgia, Pteradyktil.

Kate Ellison was born in Louisiana, grew up in Tennessee, and attended the University of Tennessee, Knoxville, graduating in 1972. At UT, she learned about feminism and began to see herself as a feminist. She has lived on wimmin's land most of the time since 1988, and has been associated with three women's land groups: Turtleland in Virginia, SPIRAL in Kentucky, and the North Forty, where she now lives, in Florida.

Kathleen "Corky" Culver has sought poetry and peace and justice, community music and dance, activism, Lesbians, sunsets and sunrises, and liberation. She was a Thoreau scholar and English professor in her spare time and takes sanctuary by lakes and women's lands.

Loba Wakinyan is a rebellious catalyst who has been setting fires to expectations from birth. Conceived, birthed, and raised in Asheville, North Carolina, Loba has a deep love of the southland, of personal "Ancestory." A current MFA student at Goddard College, Loba writes to breathe and breathes to right—for each word on the page is a political social challenge of boring and rote.

Lynn Hicks was born in Columbus, Georgia, grew up in Montgomery, Alabama, graduated from Auburn University, and taught in Atlanta before going to New York in 1970 for a master's degree in art. After seven years in the Berkshires of Massachusetts, she moved back South in 1979 for a longer gardening season. She has been a political activist since the 1970s, including participating in the SOA (School of the Americas) Watch in Columbus, Georgia, and the Selma Bridge Crossing ceremonies and Peace Walk to Montgomery, and now the Moral Monday protests in North Carolina.

Caely McHale is an undergraduate at The College of William and Mary studying English and Creative Writing.

Maria Christina Moroles (Águila) is the cofounder and president of Arco Iris Earth Care Project (AIECP), a nonprofit organization that works to fulfill the Arco Iris mission of preserving and protecting 400 acres of Ozark wilderness, in Northwest Arkansas. Águila is the matriarchal resident steward of Rancho Arco Iris, 130 acres adjacent to AIECP. Rancho was the founding home of Arco Iris and has served to provide a spiritual and environmental sanctuary, initially as a women and children of color survivors' camp. Arco Iris promotes indigenous and Ozark culture. Formerly known as Sun Hawk, she is Mexican American Indian, from the Coahuilateco Mexica nation, and she has been a *curandera*, or healer, since the age of seventeen.

Marideth Sisco, a veteran journalist, teacher, author, musician, and student of folklore, created Elder Mountain Press to publish stories of Ozarks culture and history. She holds a BFA degree from

Missouri State University and an MA from Antioch University. She hosts the public radio show, *These Ozarks Hills*, on KSMU and is finishing a novel. Sisco spent twenty years as an environmental writer for the *West Plains Quill* and was well known for her gardening column, "Crosspatch." Recently, she was consultant and featured singer in the award-winning feature film *Winter's Bone*. She helped write the soundtrack for the documentary *Stray Dog: The Movie* by the same production team.

Mary Bricker-Jenkins, daughter of a New England lady and an unfeasibly romantic gambler, traveled both of their roads until she found her own at WIT's End Farm in Tennessee. A mother, farmer, organizer, social worker, Lesbian-feminist-commie pinko old woman who cherishes southern Appalachia, she carries scores of unwritten poems and stories in the heart and has a few she wrote on her bookshelf.

Merril Mushroom grew up in Miami Beach, Florida, and came out there in the 1950s. She lived in New York City in the 1960s, and has lived in rural Middle Tennessee since the 1970s. She has written a wide variety of prose pieces. Her old-timey bar dyke stories can be found in out-of-print Lesbian publications of the 1980s and 1990s.

TeNaj McFadden was born and raised in Indiana. Since 1987 she has been back in Indiana where she managed the family farm, became disabled, and cared for her mother, who died at home from Alzheimer's disease. She is now deciding what to do with the rest of her life.

Rachel has visited several intentional communities. She feels at home in many different states in the United States. Rachel and her wife live with their three cats.

Robin Toler, ATR-BC, LAC, AIT-C, is a board-certified art therapist, licensed addictions counselor, and certified in Advanced

Integrative Therapy. Toler's practice and consulting services offer art therapy, addictions counseling, energy therapy, pain management and women's mental health. Her private practice is near Louisiana State University in Baton Rouge, Louisiana. Toler's therapy practice is based on feminist principles: equity and human rights. Toler is an artist, writer, and drummer. Contact Toler at www.robintoler.com or www.robintolerartstudio.com.

Rose Norman, a member of the Ravens Den Sanctuary land group, is a native Alabamian, now retired from college teaching. As general editor of the Southern Lesbian Feminist Activist Herstory Project, she has conducted interviews with thirty-nine Lesbians.

Susan Wiseheart was born and lived in Michigan for forty-eight years, moved to the Missouri Ozarks in 1989, and has now lived at Hawk Hill Community Land Trust for over two decades. She has been strongly influenced by antiracist work, Lesbian culture, the Michigan Womyn's Music Festival, Midwest Wimmin's Festival, many wonderful individual Lesbians, her biological family, and Old Lesbians Organizing for Change.

CONTRIBUTORS WANTED
Southern Lesbian Feminist Activist Herstory Project

Logo is signed Jennifer Weston, and we have her permission

Womonwriters continue to collaborate on a herstory of Lesbian-feminist activism in the South, particularly for the years 1968–1999. The role of Southern Lesbian-feminists in the women's movement needs to be documented before it is forgotten, and while those activists are still living. All memoirs and interviews will be archived, and some will be used in publications, with the contributors' permission and participation. The idea for this project began at Womonwrites, the Southeast Lesbian Writers' Conference, which celebrated its 37th annual spring conference in 2015 (womonwrites.wordpress.com).

For more information,
email Rose Norman at rose.norman@gmail.com
or telephone Merril Mushroom at 615-536-5287.

If you have a story to tell, or even if you might but don't know how to tell it, we would like to hear from you!.

CALLS FOR SUBMISSION

Call for Work: Performing Lesbian Feminism
Deadline: December 31, 2015

A lexis Clements is calling for writing at the intersection of performance and lesbian feminism for a special issue of *Sinister Wisdom*. At a time when queer theory and politics, popular culture, and ongoing misogyny have lead to things such as the Huffington Post's live news series hosting an extended segment focused on "The End of Lesbians," many feel not just the term lesbian but also the identities it encompasses are embattled. However, the political and theoretical legacy of lesbian feminists made significant contributions to the development of queer theory and the embodied practice of challenging gender and sexual norms, among others. Performance has long been a critical tool for lesbian feminists in celebrating, developing, and exploring ideas and identities, whether on stage, in bookstores and cafes, or even in the every day. This history includes many artists who have been involved in the WOW Cafe Theatre such as Split Britches (Peggy Shaw & Lois Weaver), Carmelita Tropicana, Holly Hughes, the Five Lesbian Brothers, and the Rivers of Honey series for queer women of color, to more contemporary work such as Allyson Mitchell's performance, installation, and collaboration Killjoy's Kastle: A Lesbian Feminist Haunted House or the ongoing cultural organizing taking place at the Esperanza Peace & Justice Center in San Antonio, Texas.

For this volume Clements is interested in exploring how artists and individuals are performing and/or drawing on lesbian feminism at this moment. How do we enact lesbian feminism today? What does the legacy of lesbian feminism mean to people creating work and living today, among those who were there for its beginnings as well as those who have chosen to take it up since then? How does it intersect with the larger umbrella of queerness and the contemporary understanding of and focus on the many variations of gender and sexuality? Can the performance of lesbian feminism today serve as a counterpoint and/or complement to the all-encompassing ethos of queerness? In what ways does performance also offer opportunities for critiques of lesbian feminism itself? Performance/script excerpts, short essays, creative non-fiction, brief memoirs, excerpts from art projects, visual art, poems, and other forms of expression are all welcome.

Please send questions and submissions to privatecommission@gmail.com. The deadline for submissions is December 31, 2015.

Alexis Clements is a performance maker, arts writer, and journalist living in Brooklyn, NY. She founded the multi-disciplinary arts project New Acquisition, and co-founded Private Commission, a queer writing group and publisher. Her creative work has been produced and published in the US and UK. Her articles, essays, and interviews have appeared in publications such as *Salon, Bitch Magazine, Autostraddle, American Theatre, The Brooklyn Rail, Two Serious Ladies, The L Magazine, Nature, Frontiers,* and *In the Flesh.* She is a regular contributor, focused on art and performance, to *Hyperallergic.* And currently she is working on a documentary film project titled ALL WE'VE GOT focused on the spaces where lesbians and queer women gather.

Call for Work: Honoring the Michigan Womyn's Music Festival
Deadline: December 31, 2015

This special issue of *Sinister Wisdom* is dedicated to honoring the forty-year phenomenon of the Michigan Womyn's Music Festival (MWMF). It celebrates MWMF as an embodiment of radical feminist separatist collaboration, transformational self-defined autonomous spaces, a commitment to sisterhood and matriarchal culture, and a musical city sprung from the earth for one week in the woods. The guest editors will curate a diversity of womyn's voices, values, traditions, and experiences of MWMF as it has changed and connected generations. We will explore what MWMF has meant to so many womyn, document its chronology, and commemorate the power of this unique community.

The guest editors are seeking submissions from writers and visual artists intimately connected with MWMF. Writers can submit poems, personal essays, short stories, oral histories, interviews, plays, and other original writing of no more than 5,000 words. Visual artists can send up to 5 paintings, drawings, photos, or other original artwork in black and white. Artists may submit one image in color for cover art consideration. All writing submissions should be in .docx, and for art, please use .jpg, .gif, or .tif (300dpi). We encourage vendors, performers, festivalgoers, facilitators, workers, and womyn from all races, ethnicities, sexualities, ages, abilities, religions, and gender identities to submit.

The guest editors welcome submissions that expand but are not limited to the following:
- Raising the Stages
- Preparing the City
- Body Acceptance
- Safety and Nudity
- Healing and Recovery
- Life Backstage
- Worker Community
- Womyn of Color
- DEAF Camping
- Pilgrimage and "Welcome Home"
- Orgasms, Sex, Romantic Love, and Exes
- Stories of Line Culture and Finally Getting In
- Growing up Gaia, Mothering the Younger Generations
- Chosen Families
- Gender Nonconforming Identities and Expressions
- Radical Spaces
- Workshops and Performances
- Finding Voice, Power, and Self
- Personal Agency in Workshifting
- Intersectional Communities
- Burlesque, Struts, and Walks and Parades
- Spirituality, Witchcraft, The Cult, and Woo
- Ecology and Nature
- Electricity, Plumbing, and Sound in the Woods
- Leather Community
- Babies and Crones

- Drugs, Fists, and Tears
- Lesbians, Lesbians, Lesbians
- Expanding Female
- Vending and Entrepreneurship
- Drum Circles, Hootenannies, Workshops with Artists
- Activism and Advocacy
- DIY Art and Culture
- Rehearsal Tent Hijinks
- RV Community
- Boys and Men

The guest editors want to preserve each submitter's voice; however, where applicable we will be adhering to *Sinister Wisdom* publishing guidelines, which follow the Chicago Manual of Style. If you are not familiar with these guidelines, please contact the editors and we will assist with any questions you may have.

The deadline for submissions is January 31, 2016; however, early submissions are encouraged and appreciated.

Please make your submissions here: https://greensubmissions.com/519/sinister-wisdom-mwmf-edition/index.php

GREENLESBIAN.COM

Lesbian-Made Art & Culture
And The Necessities of
Our Lives

MAIZE

#113
Spring 2015

Maize
A Lesbian Country Magazine

Fall 2006 $10.00   # 79

A Lesbian Country Magazine

Celebrate Lesbian Lands & Our Land Lesbian Life & Cultures

in **USA**, **$25** yearly/$15 low-income; **International $40**/ 30 in US$; **Canada $30**/ 25 in US$
Contributing more is so helpful. International best via Paypal to WomanEarthandSpirit@gmail.com
Thanks to generous subscribers sending extra, *Maize* is always, "Send **whatever you can** when and
if you can. " We want every womon to have access to *Maize!* ~ 4 wonderful big issues per year

Timeline for *Summer Maize #114* is June 21. Other issues Aug 21, Nov 21, Feb 21

Add onto my current sub _____   Start my subscription now _____   Start with issue # _____
Name: _____

Name of Land, if any: _____

Mailing address: _____

_____

Email: _____ Website _____

Birthday / anniversary (so we can celebrate you) _____

Phone: _____   cell _____

Amount Enclosed for Sub: 1 year $_____   Other $_____   **Lifetime** ($500 or more) $_____

Donation (tax deductible) : $_____ I enclose $_____ to subsidize subs for low-income wimmin

This is a Gift Subscription for _____

Message _____

Send Submissions & sub Payment in U.S. Dollars. <u>International best paid through Paypal.</u>
Check to *Maize* / Woman, Earth & Spirit ~ Paypal to *JaeHaggard@gmail.com*

Maize ~ PO Box 130 Serafina, NM 87569
JaeHaggard@gmail.com ~ *www.MaizeMagazine.org* ~ 575-421-2533

We Invite You to Be Part of Our Wondrous *AMaizing* Web!

Sinister Wisdom **Back Issues Available**

97 Out Latina Lesbians ($12)
96 What Can I Ask ($18.95)
95 Reconciliations ($12)
94 Lesbians and Exile ($12)
93 Southern Lesbian-Feminist
   Herstory 1968–94 ($12)
92 Lesbian Healthcare Workers ($12)
91 Living as a Lesbian ($17.95)
90 Catch, Quench ($12)
89 Once and Later ($12)
88 Crime Against Nature ($17.95)
87 Tribute to Adrienne Rich
86 Ignite!
85 Youth/Humor
84 Time/Space
83 Identity and Desire
82 In Amerika They Call Us
   Dykes: Lesbian Lives in the 70s
81 Lesbian Poetry – When? And
   Now!
80 Willing Up and Keeling Over
78/79 Old Lesbians/Dykes II
77 Environmental Issues Lesbian
   Concerns
76 Open Issue
75 Lesbian Theories/Lesbian
   Controversies
74 Latina Lesbians
73 The Art Issue
72 Utopia
71 Open Issue
70 30th Anniversary Celebration
68/69 Death, Grief and Surviving
67 Lesbians and Work
66 Lesbians and Activism
65 Lesbian Mothers &
   Grandmothers
64 Lesbians and Music, Drama
   and Art
63 Lesbians and Nature
62 Lesbian Writers on Reading
   and Writing *
61 Women Loving Women in
   Prison
59/60 Love, Sex & Romance
58 Open Issue
57 Healing

55 Exploring Issues of Racial &
   Sexual Identification
54 Lesbians & Religion
53 Old Dykes/Lesbians – Guest
   Edited by Lesbians Over 60
52 Allies Issue
51 New Lesbian Writing
50 Not the Ethics Issue
49 The Lesbian Body
48 Lesbian Resistance Including
   work by Dykes in Prison
47 Lesbians of Color: Tellin' It
   Like It 'Tis
46 Dyke Lives
45 Lesbians & Class (the first
   issue of a lesbian journal
   edited entirely by poverty and
   working class dykes)
43/44 15th Anniversary double-size
   (368 pgs) retrospective
41 Italian American Women's Issue
40 Friendship
39 Disability
36 Surviving Psychiatric Assault/
   Creating emotional well being
35 Passing
34 Sci-Fi, Fantasy & Lesbian Visions
33 Wisdom
32 Open Issue
               *Available on audio tape

Back issues are $6.00
unless noted plus $3.00
Shipping & Handling
for 1st issue; $1.00 for each
additional issue.
Order online at
www.sinisterwisdom.org

Or mail check or money
order to:
Sinister Wisdom
PO Box 3252
Berkeley, CA 94703